PLANTS, ALGAE, AND FUNGI

Britannica Illustrated Science Library

Encyclopædia Britannica, Inc.

Chicago ▪ London ▪ New Delhi ▪ Paris ▪ Seoul ▪ Sydney ▪ Taipei ▪ Tokyo

Britannica Illustrated Science Library

Idea and Concept of This Work: Editorial Sol 90

Project Management: Fabián Cassan

Photo Credits: Corbis, William Manning/Corbis, ESA, Getty Images, Graphic News, NASA, National Geographic, Science Photo Library

Illustrators: Guido Arroyo, Pablo Aschei, Gustavo J. Caironi, Hernán Cañellas, Leonardo César, José Luis Corsetti, Vanina Farías, Joana Garrido, Celina Hilbert, Isidro López, Diego Martín, Jorge Martínez, Marco Menco, Ala de Mosca, Diego Mourelos, Eduardo Pérez, Javier Pérez, Ariel Piroyansky, Ariel Roldán, Marcel Socías, Néstor Taylor, Trebol Animation, Juan Venegas, Coralia Vignau, 3DN, 3DOM studio, Jorge Ivanovich, Fernando Ramallo, Constanza Vicco, Diego Mourelos

Composition and Pre-press Services: Editorial Sol 90
Translation Services and Index: Publication Services, Inc.

Britannica Illustrated Science Library Staff

Editorial
Michael Levy, *Executive Editor, Core Editorial*
John Rafferty, *Associate Editor, Earth Sciences*
William L. Hosch, *Associate Editor, Mathematics and Computers*
Kara Rogers, *Associate Editor, Life Sciences*
Rob Curley, *Senior Editor, Science and Technology*
David Hayes, *Special Projects Editor*

Art and Composition
Steven N. Kapusta, *Director*
Carol A. Gaines, *Composition Supervisor*
Christine McCabe, *Senior Illustrator*

Media Acquisition
Kathy Nakamura, *Manager*

Copy Department
Sylvia Wallace, *Director*
Julian Ronning, *Supervisor*

Information Management and Retrieval
Sheila Vasich, *Information Architect*

Production Control
Marilyn L. Barton

Manufacturing
Kim Gerber, *Director*

Encyclopædia Britannica, Inc.

Jacob E. Safra, *Chairman of the Board*

Jorge Aguilar-Cauz, *President*

Michael Ross, *Senior Vice President, Corporate Development*

Dale H. Hoiberg, *Senior Vice President and Editor*

Marsha Mackenzie, *Director of Production*

International Standard Book Number (set):
  978-1-59339-382-3
International Standard Book Number (volume):
  978-1-59339-394-6
Britannica Illustrated Science Library:
  Plants, Algae, and Fungi 2008

Printed in China

www.britannica.com

Plants, Algae, and Fungi

Contents

Grain of mallow pollen, magnified 600 times, pictured on page 1. Pollen's function is to fertilize the female organs of the plant, a task that is achieved with the help of bees.

Green Revolution

RICE CROP
Rice is synonymous with food security in much of Asia. It is also a staple food in western Africa, the Caribbean, and the tropical regions of Latin America.

There are approximately 300,000 plant species in the world, and they live in a variety of regions, from the frozen Arctic tundra to the lush tropical rainforests. Without plants we would not be able to live; they have always been intimately linked to life on Earth. Thanks to photosynthesis, plants provide us with food, medicines, wood, resins, and oxygen, among other things. Discovering plants' processes for converting sunlight into carbohydrates such as sugars and starches is almost magical. It is marvelous to understand how an organism that cannot move learned to maximize the energy that it receives from the Sun, as well as to discover the mechanisms that enable it to face so many different environmental challenges. Some leaves have essential adaptations, such as thick skin, thorns, or fleshy stalks, which allow them to survive in very dry environments. Others, such as the tomato plant, form certain proteins when temperatures drop in order to protect themselves from damage caused by freezing.

You may be surprised to learn why plants invest so much energy and effort into producing flowers. In this book we will describe for you in detail, step by step, how fertilization takes place. Did you know that pollination is aided by the wind and insects and that some flowers can be pollinated only by a certain species of insect? You will find all this and much more in the pages of this book, which includes spectacular images and illustrations that give an inside view of the core of a tree and even show the functions of its tissues and the veins of its leaves.

What were the first plants to conquer the Earth like, and how did they help convert bare rock into soil? What happened next, and which species evolved and spread worldwide during the Carboniferous Period? A complete historical overview of plants is included in this book, as is an explanation of the radical differences between plants, algae, and fungi—the latter two of which are now considered to be more closely related to animals than to plants. Although the place of plants in the human diet is nothing new, the search for other beneficial uses of plants is a more modern development. Crops— such as rice, corn, wheat, rye, barley, oats, soy, lentils, and chickpeas—are grown worldwide as sources of proteins, vitamins, minerals, and other nutrients necessary for our bodies to function, and they also provide people with an important source of income. ●

Background

According to scientific evidence, the nearest relatives of plants are algae that lived on the shores of lagoons. Later, from these habitats, which were at times dry and at times damp, the first land plants emerged. Most had to adapt in order to prosper in a different environment. Such adaptation enabled them to achieve

GIANT SEQUOIA
Some trees of this species are found in central California.

amazing growth, as exemplified by the giant sequoia *(Sequoiadendron giganteum)*, which can measure 260 feet (80 m) tall and 100 feet (30 m) in circumference at its base. Did you know that plants grow bigger as their cells multiply and expand? Many can grow 0.4 inch (1 cm) per day, and their growth can create enough pressure to open cracks in asphalt. ●

Kingdoms of the Quiet Life

Representing a vast array of life-forms, the plant kingdom includes approximately 300,000 species. Their most outstanding feature is the presence of chloroplasts with chlorophyll, a pigment that enables them to transform solar energy into chemical energy. They use this energy to produce their food. Plants need to attach themselves to a substrate (usually the ground), from which they can extract water and nutrients. This attachment, however, also keeps them from moving from place to place. Algae and fungi were once included in the plant kingdom, but they are now considered to be separate from plants and to belong to the kingdoms Protista and Fungi, respectively. ●

MOSS
Sphagnum sp.

RED MARINE ALGA
Rhodomela sp.

Algae

are commonly considered water plants, but this is not the case. Algae have neither roots nor stalks. Because they live in the water (freshwater or salt water), they need no substrate. Some are microscopic, but large algae formations can be found in the ocean. Algae are classified into families depending on their color. Together green algae and plants make up the group of organisms called the "green line," whose members are characterized by having chloroplasts and by storing grains of starch in the cytoplasm as a reserve.

Bryophytes

include mosses and worts. Mosses have rhizoids rather than roots. They can also absorb water through their entire body surface. Bryophytes lack a means of surviving long periods of drought. When dry periods come, bryophytes enter a latent state. Because they have no system of veins for transporting nutrients, they can barely grow beyond 0.4 inch (1 cm) long. In order to reproduce they need to be near liquid water.

Plants

The plant kingdom (Plantae) includes organisms whose characteristics include the presence of the pigment chlorophyll to convert solar energy into chemical energy for producing food from water and carbon dioxide. This ability is called autotrophy. All plants, whether large or small, play an extremely important role in providing food for all other living beings. Plants cannot move from place to place, but their gametes, spores (cells that separate from a plant and can germinate), and seeds can move about, especially with the help of water and wind.

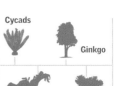

Green Algae

Bryophytes (Mosses)

Horsetail Rushes

Psilophyta

Club Mosses

Ferns

Cycads

Ginkgo

Gnetophyta

Conifers

Anthophyta or Flowering Plants

SEEDLESS

WITH SEEDS

WITHOUT VEINS

WITH VEINS

PLANTS

FERN
Osmunda sp.

Seedless

Ferns are the most common seedless plants today. Many are thought to have originated during the Devonian Period and reached their greatest splendor in the Carboniferous Period. Their tissues are simpler than those of plants with seeds, and their green stems have a large surface area, giving them a great capacity for photosynthesis. Ferns need water so that they can reproduce by means of spores. The spores are produced in spore cases called sporangia, which grow on leaves called sporophylls.

FERNS
are the most diverse group of seedless plants. Their origin dates back to the Devonian Period.

SPIKE MOSS
has scalelike leaves, some of which are clustered in the form of a spike.

PSILOPHYTA
are extremely simple plants; they lack roots and true leaves, but they have a stalk with veins.

HORSETAIL RUSHES
have roots, stems, and true leaves. The leaves are small and encircle the stems.

CONIFERS

are the most abundant plants with seeds today. Their reproductive structures are called cones. Most conifers are evergreens.

CYCADS

are tropical plants that look like palm trees. Their reproduction is similar to that of pine trees, but they are dioecious (each plant has flowers of only one sex).

GINKGOS

Only one species is left in this group, which is the oldest genus of living trees.

GNETOPHYTA

Plants with naked seeds and a vascular system similar to that of angiosperms

Gymnosperma

The Greek word means "naked seed." Gymnosperms are vascular plants with exposed seeds and no flowers. Ginkgos (Ginkgophyta) and cycads (Cycadophyta) were the most common plant groups in ancient times. Today conifers (such as pines, larches, cypresses, and firs) are the most common type. Conifers are monoicous—that is, the same plant has both male and female sexual organs—and their seeds are held between the scales of a structure called a cone.

SITKA SPRUCE
Picea sitchensis

Fungi

belong to a different kingdom from that of plants. Fungi, unlike plants, do not carry out photosynthesis, and they store energy in the form of glycogen rather than starch. Fungi are heterotrophic (they get their food from other organisms), and they take in food by absorption. Fungi can be either parasitic or feed on dead organic material. Some fungi are microscopic; others are large and conspicuous. Their bodies are composed of a mycelium, a mass of filaments called hyphae. Some fungi also have a fruit-bearing structure.

WHITE MUSHROOM
Agaricus bisporus

WHEAT
Triticum sp.

Angiosperms

have seeds, flowers, and fruit. They include more than 250,000 species and are adapted to nearly all environments except for Antarctica. They reproduce sexually by producing flowers that later form fruits with seeds. Angiosperms have an efficient vascular system for transporting water (through the xylem) and food (through the phloem). Angiosperms make up a division of the plant kingdom that includes plants with bright flowers; grains, such as rice and wheat; other crops, such as cotton, tobacco, and coffee; and trees, such as oak, cherry, and chestnut.

ORCHIDS

have many petals; their number of petals is always a multiple of three. This makes them, along with cereal grains, monocotyledons (monocots).

ORCHID
Cattleya trianae

CEREALS

are monocotyledons. Their seeds have only one cotyledon (embryonic leaf), and their mature leaves have parallel veins.

Aquatic Plants

These plants are especially adapted for living in ponds, streams, lakes, and rivers—places where other land plants cannot grow. Although aquatic plants belong to many different families, they have similar adaptations and are therefore an example of adaptive convergence. They include submerged plants and floating plants; plants that may or may not be rooted at the bottom; amphibious plants, which have leaves both above and below the water's surface; and heliophilic plants, which have only their roots underwater. ●

A Vital Role

Aquatic plants play an important role in the ecosystem not only for crustaceans, insects, and worms but also for fish, birds, and mammals because they are an important source of food and shelter for these categories of animals. Aquatic plants also play a major role in converting solar energy into the organic materials upon which many living things depend.

Rooted Plants with Floating Leaves

Such plants are often found in standing or slow-moving water. They have fixed rhizomes and petiolate leaves (leaves with a stalk that connects to a stem) that float on the surface of the water. Some of the plants have submerged leaves, some have floating leaves, and some have leaves outside the water, with each type having a different shape. In the case of floating leaves the properties of the upper surface are different from those of the lower surface, which is in contact with the water.

PARROT FEATHER
Myriophyllum aquaticum
This plant is native to temperate, subtropical, and tropical regions, and it is highly effective at oxygenating water.

TROPICAL WATER LILY
Victoria cruciana
It grows in deep, calm waters. Its leaves can measure up to 7 feet (2 m) across.

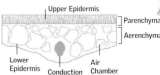

Floating Leaves
The rhizomes are fixed, the leaves grow on long stalks, and the leaf surface floats on the water.

- Upper Epidermis
- Parenchyma
- Aerenchyma
- Lower Epidermis
- Conduction Bundle
- Air Chamber

YELLOW FLOATING HEART
Nymphoides peltata
It produces small creased yellow flowers all summer long.

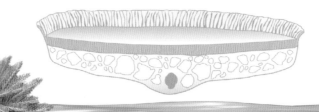

Rooted Underwater Plants

The entire plant is submerged. The small root system serves only to anchor the plant since the stem can directly absorb water, carbon dioxide, and minerals. These plants are often found in flowing water. The submerged stems have no system of support—the water holds up the plant.

SAGO PONDWEED
Potamogeton densus
This water plant can be found in shallow depressions of clear-flowing streams.

HORNWORT
Ceratophyllum sp.
This plant has an abundance of fine leaves that form a conelike structure on each stem.

They produce and release oxygen as a result of photosynthesis.

Aquatic but Modern

The evolutionary history of plants began in water environments. They later conquered land by means of structures such as roots. Modern aquatic plants are not a primitive group, however. On the contrary, they have returned to the water environment by acquiring highly specialized organs and tissues. For example, some tissues have air pockets that enable the plant to float.

Aerenchyma

is always found in floating organisms. This tissue has an extensive system of intercellular spaces through which gases are diffused.

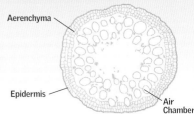

- Aerenchyma
- Epidermis
- Air Chamber

Submerged stems have no support system because the water holds up the plant. Their limiting factor is oxygen availability, so the aerenchyma helps make this substance available to the plant.

Amphibious or Wetland Plants

These species live on the edges of ponds, rivers, and swamps. They are also found in salt marshes, which are periodically flooded by tides or river overflows. These plants are a transition between aquatic and land plants. Their limiting factor is the availability of oxygen, so they have well-developed aerenchyma.

300 THE NUMBER OF WELL-KNOWN SPECIES OF WATER PLANTS

CATTAILS
Typha sp.
grow in moist soil, around lake margins, and in marshes in both temperate and tropical climates.

ARROWHEAD
Sagittaria sagittifolia
Its flowers, with three white petals and purple stamens, form during the summer.

LACHENALIA
Lachenalia viridiflora
This plant is attractive, with a large number of flowers.

Aquatic plant with especially beautiful flowers.

The roots and rhizomes under the water are well developed.

KNOTWEED
Polygonum sp.
This aquatic plant grows in marshy vegetation.

BLADDERWORT
Utricularia vulgaris
These carnivorous plants complement their diet with small aquatic creatures.

Submerged or Free

Some underwater plants are free, without roots, but with developed stalks and divided leaves. Other floating plants have a rosette shape and leaves modified for floating; they have well-developed roots with root caps but without absorbent hairs. The roots help the plant to stay balanced on top of the water.

Pneumatophores
are floating roots that are involved in air exchange. They take oxygen from the surface, and it circulates to the rest of the plant through its intracellular spaces. They probably also allow carbon dioxide to escape. Certain plants have a special adaptation that consists of air sacs that store oxygen for periods when the plant will be submerged or that speed up the plant's transpiration.

The underwater parts do not have an impermeable outer layer, so they can absorb minerals and gases directly from the water.

EELGRASS
Vallisneria sp.
This oxygenating plant is found in ponds and aquariums.

Conquest of Land

The movement of plants from shallow water onto land is associated with a series of evolutionary events. Certain changes in the genetic makeup of plants enabled them to face the new and extreme conditions found on the Earth's surface. Although land habitats offered plants direct exposure to sunlight, they also presented the problem of transpiration and the loss of water that it produces. This difficulty had to be overcome before plants could spread over land. ●

Vital Changes

Roots are among the most important adaptations for plants' success in land habitats. Root systems anchor the plant in the substrate and serve as a pathway for water and mineral nutrients to enter it. Besides roots, the development of a cuticle (skin membrane) to cover the entire plant's surface was crucial. Cells in the epidermis produce this waterproof membrane, which helps the plant tolerate the heat generated by sunlight and the wear and loss of water caused by the wind. This protection is interrupted by pores, which allow for gas exchange.

Green Revolution

Leaves are the main organs for photosynthesis in land plants. After plants appeared on land more than 440 million years ago, the amount of photosynthesis taking place gradually increased. This increase is believed to be one of the reasons the concentration of carbon dioxide in the atmosphere decreased. As a result, the Earth's average temperature also decreased.

50,000

SPECIES OF FUNGUS LIVE ALONGSIDE LAND-DWELLING PLANTS.

MALE FERN
Dryopteris filix-mas
These vascular plants need liquid water to reproduce.

MOSS
Sphagnum sp.
Bryophytes are the simplest of all land plants.

Epiphytes

grow on plants or on some other supporting surface. Their anatomy includes secondary adaptations that enable them to live without being in contact with the soil.

Grasses

take advantage of long hours of summer daylight to grow and reproduce. Their stalks do not have reinforcing tissues that would enable them to remain erect.

**STEMLESS
SOW THISTLE**
Sonchus acaulis
These plants lack a stem.

SWEET VIOLET
Viola odorata
This plant's spring flowers have a pleasant scent.

Giants

Trees are distinguished by their woody trunks. As a tree grows from a tender shoot, it develops a tissue that gives it strength, enabling it to grow over 330 feet (100 m) tall. Trees are found in the principal terrestrial ecosystems.

CHESTNUTS
Castanea sp.

WALNUTS
Juglans sp.

BEECHES
Fagus sp.

MAPLES
Acer sp.

OAKS
Quercus sp.

LINDENS
Tilia sp.

360 Feet
(110 M)
**THE HEIGHT REACHED BY SOME
SEQUOIA SEMPERVIREN TREES**

Anatomy of a Tree

The oak tree is the undisputed king of the Western world. It is known for its lobed leaves and the large cap of its acorn, a nut found on all trees of the genus *Quercus*. The tree's main trunk grows upward and branches out toward the top. Oaks are a large group, containing many types of deciduous trees. Under optimal conditions oaks can grow to a height of more than 130 feet (40 m) and live an average of 600 years. ●

The leaves absorb CO$_2$ and produce sugars by means of photosynthesis.

Transpiration (the loss of water vapor) in the leaves pulls the xylem sap upward.

Climate

Trees grow in any place where there is sufficient water in the soil.

Flowers

The tree produces hanging male flowers, whereas female flowers are hidden among the leaves.

Buds

are formed by protective scales that fall off in the spring. They grow into new leaves and branches.

Summer
The oak blossoms. It increases in height, and its trunk grows thicker.

Winter
The leaves fall away; the tree is dormant until spring.

Spring
The cycle begins as the first leaves appear.

Autumn
Low temperatures weaken the branches.

Oak-Tree Products

The bark is rich in tannin, which is used in curing leather and as an astringent. The wood is strong and resists rotting.

The xylem transports water and minerals from the roots to the rest of the tree.

The phloem transports sugars from the leaves to the rest of the tree.

Energy Source
The chlorophyll traps energy from sunlight and uses it to convert water and carbon dioxide into food.

Surface
Mosses use the bark of oak trees as a source of moisture.

grow sideways to form a deep, broad root system.

Absorption of Water and Minerals

Woodpeckers drill holes in the tree with their beaks as they look for insects.

Spring
New leaves begin to replace the old ones.

Winter
The leaf falls away, and the tree remains dormant.

Autumn
The cells at the end of each leaf stem weaken.

Beginnings
In its first year of life an oak tree's roots can grow nearly 5 feet (1.5 m).

600 years
THE AVERAGE LIFE SPAN OF AN OAK

Trunk
The trunk is strong and grows straight upward. The top of the tree widens with branches, which may be twisted, knotted, or bent.

Summer
The leaves undertake photosynthesis, and the rest of the tree uses the sugars it produces.

Leaves
are arranged one leaf to a stem on alternating sides of the twig. They have rounded lobes on either side of the main vein.

Acorns
have dark stripes along their length. Their caps have flat scales.

Seeds
Some species have sweet-tasting seeds; others are bitter.

— Achene: A hard seed that does not split open at maturity

— Remains of the Carpel (female reproductive part)

Growth Rings

Bark

Feeding on Light

An important characteristic of plants is their ability to use sunlight and the carbon dioxide in the air to manufacture their own complex nutrients. This process, called photosynthesis, takes place in chloroplasts, cellular components that contain the necessary enzyme machinery to transform solar energy into chemical energy. Each plant cell can have between 20 and 100 oval-shaped chloroplasts. Chloroplasts can reproduce themselves, suggesting that they were once autonomous organisms that established a symbiosis, which produced the first plant cell. ●

Why Green?

Leaves absorb energy from visible light, which consists of different colors. The leaves reflect only the green light.

Leaves

are made of several types of plant tissues. Some serve as a support, and some serve as filler material.

Algae

perform photosynthesis underwater. Together with water plants, they provide most of the atmosphere's oxygen.

O_2 IS RELEASED BY PLANTS INTO THE EARTH'S ATMOSPHERE

Plant Cells

have three traits that differentiate them from animal cells: cell walls (which are made up of 40 percent cellulose), a large vacuole containing water and trace mineral elements, and chloroplasts containing chlorophyll. Like an animal cell, a plant cell has a nucleus.

CHLOROPHYLL
is the most abundant pigment in leaves.

WATER
Photosynthesis requires a constant supply of water, which reaches the leaves through the plant's roots and stem.

Cell Membrane

Cell Wall

Plant Tissues

The relative stiffness of plant cells is provided by cellulose, the polysaccharide formed by the plant's cell walls. This substance is made of thousands of glucose units, and it is very difficult to hydrolyze (break down in water).

CARBON DIOXIDE
is absorbed by plant cells to form sugars by means of photosynthesis.

OXYGEN
is a by-product of photosynthesis. It exits the surface of the leaves through their stoma (two-celled pores).

Vacuole
provides water and pressure and gives the cell consistency.

Stages of the Process

Photosynthesis takes place in two stages. The first, called photosystem II, depends directly on the amount of light received, which causes the chlorophyll to release electrons. The resulting gaps are filled by electrons of water, which breaks down and releases oxygen and ionized hydrogen (2H+).

1 ATP formation is powered by the movement of electrons into receptor molecules in a chain of oxidation and reduction reactions.

2 In photosystem I light energy is absorbed, sending electrons into other receptors and making NADPH out of NADP+.

3 The ATP and NADPH obtained are the net gain of the system, in addition to oxygen. Two water molecules are split apart in the process, but one is regenerated when the ATP is formed.

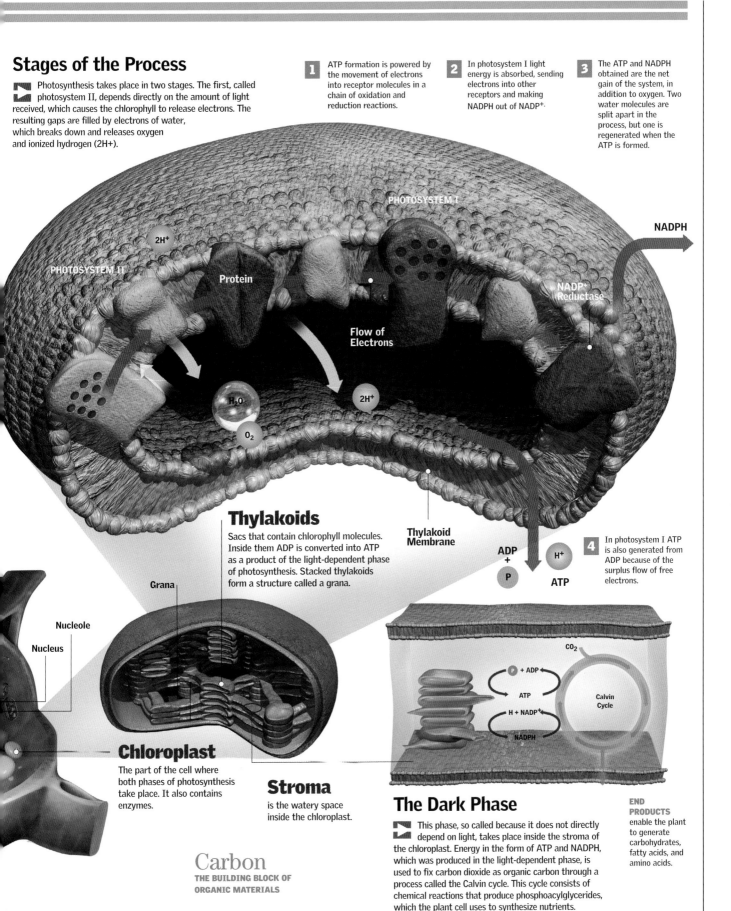

PHOTOSYSTEM I

PHOTOSYSTEM II

2H+

Protein

Flow of Electrons

H₂O₂

O₂

2H+

NADPH

NADP⁺ Reductase

Thylakoids

Sacs that contain chlorophyll molecules. Inside them ADP is converted into ATP as a product of the light-dependent phase of photosynthesis. Stacked thylakoids form a structure called a grana.

Grana

Thylakoid Membrane

ADP + P

H⁺

ATP

4 In photosystem I ATP is also generated from ADP because of the surplus flow of free electrons.

Nucleole

Nucleus

CO₂

P + ADP

ATP

H + NADP⁺

NADPH

Calvin Cycle

Chloroplast

The part of the cell where both phases of photosynthesis take place. It also contains enzymes.

Stroma

is the watery space inside the chloroplast.

The Dark Phase

This phase, so called because it does not directly depend on light, takes place inside the stroma of the chloroplast. Energy in the form of ATP and NADPH, which was produced in the light-dependent phase, is used to fix carbon dioxide as organic carbon through a process called the Calvin cycle. This cycle consists of chemical reactions that produce phosphoacylglycerides, which the plant cell uses to synthesize nutrients.

END PRODUCTS enable the plant to generate carbohydrates, fatty acids, and amino acids.

Carbon
THE BUILDING BLOCK OF ORGANIC MATERIALS

From Algae to Ferns

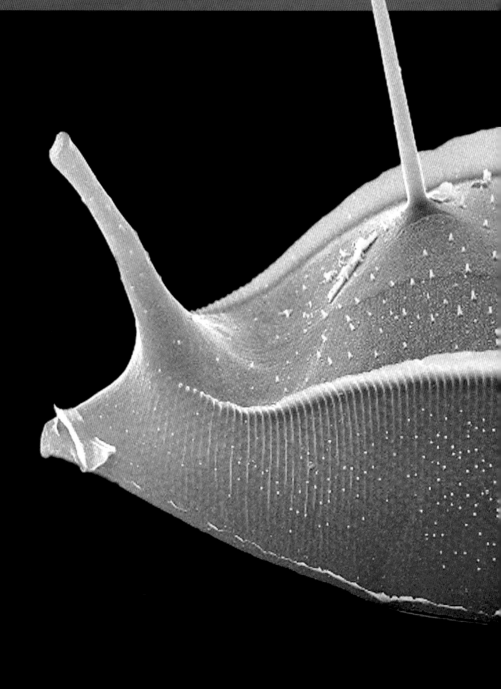

Algae (including seaweed) do not belong to the plant kingdom, because they do not have all the characteristics and functions of plants. Algae have neither roots nor stems. Because they live in water, they do not need these structures for absorbing water. Algae grow on the sea floor or on the surface of rocks in the ocean, in rivers, and in

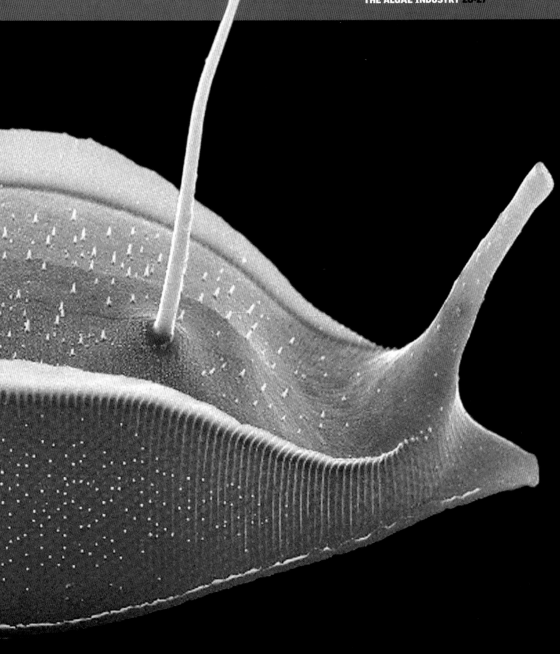

DIATOMACEOUS ALGAE
The scientific name of this type of single-celled algae is *Biddulphia laevis*. It is usually found close to the surface of very shallow bodies of water.

lakes. Their shape and color are extremely varied. The annual world harvest of algae is estimated at more than 1 million tons in dry weight. Asian countries (Japan and China) produce 80 percent of the world's harvest. Algae are used in agriculture, the food industry, pharmaceuticals, preservatives, and medicine. They are an important source of income for many workers. ●

Colors of Life

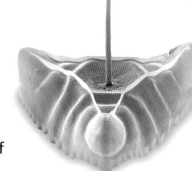

Algae are living things that manufacture their own food using photosynthesis. Their color is related to this process, and it has been used as a way of classifying them. They are also grouped according to the number of cells they have. There are many kinds of one-celled algae. Some algae form colonies, and others have multicellular bodies. Some types of brown seaweed can reach a length of more than 150 feet (45 m). ●

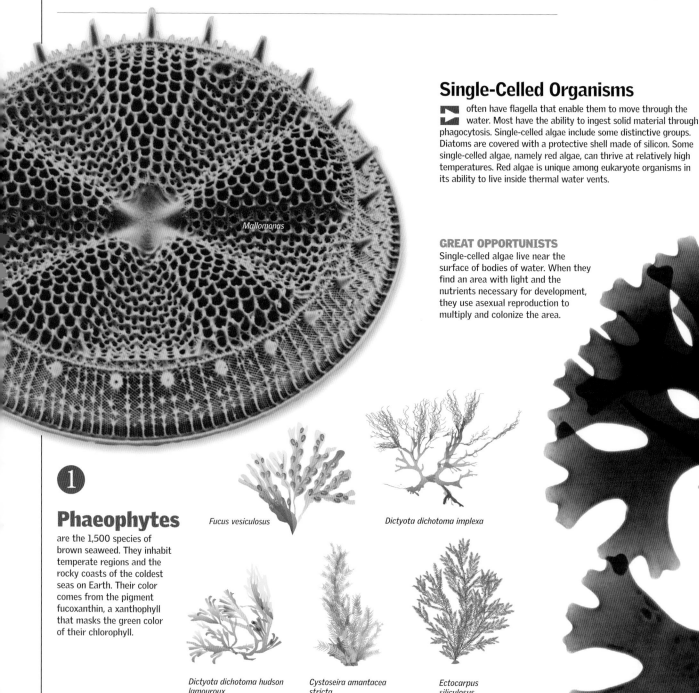

Mallomonas

Single-Celled Organisms

often have flagella that enable them to move through the water. Most have the ability to ingest solid material through phagocytosis. Single-celled algae include some distinctive groups. Diatoms are covered with a protective shell made of silicon. Some single-celled algae, namely red algae, can thrive at relatively high temperatures. Red algae is unique among eukaryote organisms in its ability to live inside thermal water vents.

GREAT OPPORTUNISTS
Single-celled algae live near the surface of bodies of water. When they find an area with light and the nutrients necessary for development, they use asexual reproduction to multiply and colonize the area.

1

Phaeophytes
are the 1,500 species of brown seaweed. They inhabit temperate regions and the rocky coasts of the coldest seas on Earth. Their color comes from the pigment fucoxanthin, a xanthophyll that masks the green color of their chlorophyll.

Fucus vesiculosus

Dictyota dichotoma implexa

Dictyota dichotoma hudson lamouroux

Cystoseira amantacea stricta

Ectocarpus siliculosus

Multicelled Organisms

This group of algae includes multicelled structures. They form colonies with mobile, single-celled algae that group together more or less regularly in a shared mucilaginous capsule. They can also appear in threadlike shapes, which branch off, or in bulky shapes, which are made up of layers of cells with a particular degree of cellular differentiation, that together are called a thallus.

Scenedesmus quadricauda

Micrasteria rotata

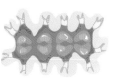

Micrasteria staurastrum

Acetabularia crenulata

Pinnularia borealis

② Chlorophytes

constitute the group of green algae. The majority of species are microscopic, single-celled organisms with flagella. Others form into filaments, and yet others form large multicellular bodies. The group Ulvophyceae includes sea lettuce, which resembles a leaf of lettuce and is edible. The group Charophyceae includes stoneworts, which contain calcium carbonate deposits. The chlorophytes are linked evolutionarily with plants because they contain the same forms of chlorophyll, and their cell walls contain cellulose.

Chlamydomonas

6,000
DIFFERENT SPECIES
have been classified within this group
of green algae, or chlorophytes.

③ Rhodophytes

are characterized by their phycoerythrin pigments, which give the algae a reddish color by masking their chlorophyll's green color. Most rhodophytes grow below the intertidal zone near tropical and subtropical coasts. They are distributed throughout the principal oceans of the world and grow mainly in shaded areas in warm, calm water.

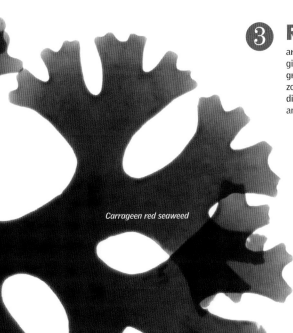

Carrageen red seaweed

Hypoglossum hypoglossoides

Bangia atropurpurea

Nitophyllum punctatum

Halymenia floresia

Apoglossum ruscifolium

How Algae Reproduce

The reproduction of algae can be sexual or asexual in alternating phases, depending on the species and on environmental conditions. Vegetative multiplication occurs through fragmentation or through the production of spores. In sexual reproduction the fertilization of the gametes (sexual cells) produces a zygote that will give rise to a new alga. During asexual reproduction there is no genetic exchange, and the algae produced are clones of the original. Sexual reproduction, in contrast, produces algae with new characteristics that may help them to better adapt to their environment. ●

Asexual

Asexual reproduction does not involve fertilization. It can take place in either of two ways. In fragmentation, segments of an alga become detached from its body, and, since the alga does not have any specialized organs, the segments continue to grow as long as environmental conditions remain favorable. The other form of asexual reproduction is by means of spores, special cells that form from a normal cell. Some algae spores have one or more filaments, or flagella, that allow the alga to swim freely. When the appropriate environmental conditions are found, the spores germinate into new algae.

ZOOSPORE
A structure that can produce a new individual asexually

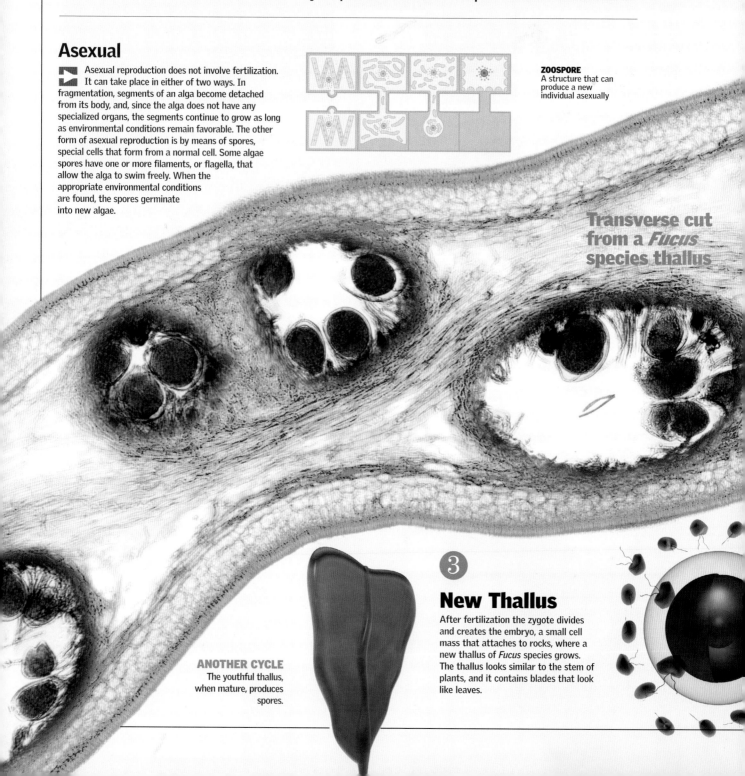

Transverse cut from a *Fucus* species thallus

ANOTHER CYCLE
The youthful thallus, when mature, produces spores.

3

New Thallus

After fertilization the zygote divides and creates the embryo, a small cell mass that attaches to rocks, where a new thallus of *Fucus* species grows. The thallus looks similar to the stem of plants, and it contains blades that look like leaves.

Sexual

Sporophytes generate spores in every species of microscopic algae. New individuals born from these spores are called gametophytes, and they produce gametes, which can be male, female, or hermaphrodite. During fertilization the male gametes (antheridia) and the female ones (ovum) form a cell called a zygote, which develops into a new thallus when it grows. Gametocytes and sporophytes can vary in morphology. If they are similar, they are called isomorphic, and if they are different, they are called heteromorphic.

MALE FUCUS
The male fucus has receptacles in which antheridia form.

1

Antheridium

The male gametangia (structure that produces gametes). They produce antherozoids, which have two flagellae and are smaller than the ovum, or female gamete. They swim until they reach an ovum and then surround it.

JOURNEY
Once they become detached, antherozoids use their flagella to move in the water.

1

Ovum

In the reproductive stage female gametangia form at the tips of the thalluses. This is where the female sexual cells (ova) develop.

OPENING
The sac that contains the ovum opens.

2

Fertilization

Both fertilization and asexual reproduction are the natural means of perpetuation for this species. Algae form new individuals similar to themselves through reproduction. When an antherozoid penetrates the ovum, it fertilizes the egg and forms a zygote.

APPROACH
The journey of the antherozoids coincides with the opening of the female gametangia.

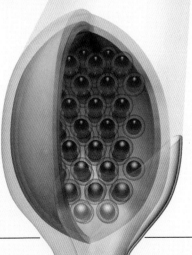

FEMALE FUCUS
The receptacles secrete a greenish gelatin made up of female gametes. The gametes are freed when the sac that contains them breaks.

Terrestrial and Marine Algae

As long as there is water, the survival of an alga is assured. Algae are found both in the oceans and in freshwater, but not all can survive in both environments. Depth, temperature, and salt concentrations of water are characteristics that determine whether algae can live in a given area. Algae can be green, brown, or red. Of the three, red algae are found in the deepest waters. Some species of algae can live outside of water, but they are nevertheless found in humid places, such as in mud or on stone walls or rocks. ●

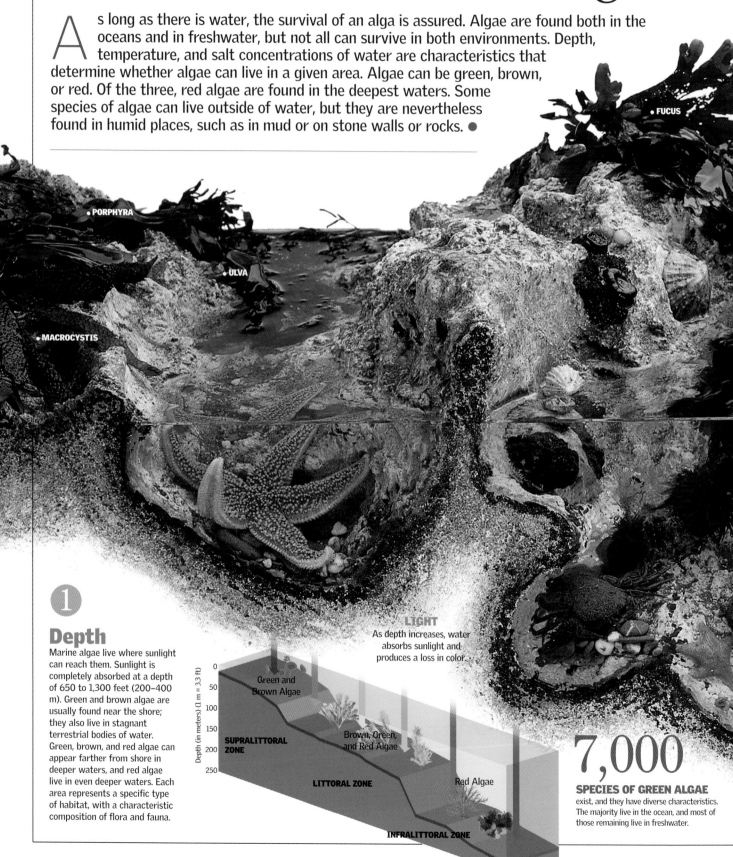

• FUCUS

• PORPHYRA

• ULVA

• MACROCYSTIS

① Depth

Marine algae live where sunlight can reach them. Sunlight is completely absorbed at a depth of 650 to 1,300 feet (200–400 m). Green and brown algae are usually found near the shore; they also live in stagnant terrestrial bodies of water. Green, brown, and red algae can appear farther from shore in deeper waters, and red algae live in even deeper waters. Each area represents a specific type of habitat, with a characteristic composition of flora and fauna.

LIGHT
As depth increases, water absorbs sunlight and produces a loss in color.

Depth (in meters) (1 m = 3.3 ft)

0
50
100
150
200
250

Green and Brown Algae

SUPRALITTORAL ZONE

Brown, Green, and Red Algae

LITTORAL ZONE

Red Algae

INFRALITTORAL ZONE

7,000

SPECIES OF GREEN ALGAE
exist, and they have diverse characteristics. The majority live in the ocean, and most of those remaining live in freshwater.

② Concentration of Salts

The waters that cover the Earth's surface are classified into two types: salt water, which forms the oceans and seas, and freshwater, or continental water. Marine water has a concentration of dissolved salts that is generally considered to be uniform. In contrast, the salt concentration of continental water can vary from place to place, causing it to have a different effect on living organisms.

MARINE WATER

Salts	%
Ca^{2+}	1.2
Mg^{2+}	3.7
Na^+	30.6
K^+	1.1
Cl^-	55.1
SO_4^{2-}	7.7
HCO_3^-	0.4

FRESHWATER

Salts	%
Ca^{2+}	17
Mg^{2+}	3.4
Na^+	3.0
K^+	1.8
Cl^-	3.3
SO_4^{2-}	8.2
HCO_3^-	63.5

● PORPHYRA

● MACROCYSTIS

● ULVA

● CODIUM

EARTH

Less Incidence

SUN

More Incidence

Less Incidence

③ Water Temperature

Temperature, which varies according to latitude and marine currents, plays an important role in determining where algae can live. The energy that the Sun's radiation provides to the oceans varies with its angle of incidence, but currents and tides distribute this energy. Ocean temperature is also dependent on depth—as the depth increases, the temperature decreases.

The Algae Industry

I n China algae have been used for food, as well as for traditional medicine, for thousands of years. However, the algae industry began on a broad scale in the 17th century in Japan with the production of caustic soda and potassium hydroxide from the ashes of brown algae. A century later Western countries began to exploit algae in order to extract iodine and other chemical compounds of great economic value, such as phycocolloids (gelatin-like substances that can be obtained from several species of algae). The most commonly used phycocolloids are agar, carrageenan, and algin. ●

How Agar Is Obtained

Most algae collection is still done by hand, although commonly used large species, such as the Caribbean Sargasso, are also collected with special boats in which processing of the algae can begin. The first stages, especially drying, are typically carried out by natural methods, but large fire-heated drying drums are used in some countries of Europe and North America. Although the use of heated drums is more expensive, it can result in a product of higher quality.

1.5
TONS PER DAY
The amount of *Gelidium* algae extractd by hand in Japan.

DRY ALGAE
Properly processed, gelatin can be obtained from these algae.

FILTERING
The noxious residues are eliminated. Then the algae are filtered and transported to a tank.

FILTER

POOL
The pool receives t mixture free from rock or shell matte and a mechanism i the tank slowly sti the mixture.

REGENERATION
In order for the algae to grow back, only 40 percent of it is harvested.

Dulse
Palmaria sp.

START
The algae are given an alkaline pH.

WASHING
They are washed with water; then acid is added.

COOKING
The mass is cooked with a pH of 6.5 or 7.

DRYING
prevents the algae from rotting. Algae are first washed with seawater.

COLLECTION
Large algae are collected with cranes from a boat; small algae are collected by hand or with rakes.

ALGAE BUNDLE
If the algae are dried properly, they can be stored for years.

BASINS
can withstand high temperatures. In the last basin the mass is cooked at 212° F (100° C).

13 feet
(4 M)
The depth at which Sargasso is collected.

①

Alkalinization

After the dry bundles are gathered, the algae are transported to an alkaline treatment pond. There sodium hydroxide (NaOH) is added, and the mixture is heated to a temperature of 176° F (80° C). The mixture is then washed and hydrated with cold water.

②

Washing and Bleaching

After the alkaline treatment algae pass through a process in which they are washed with cold water. To ensure an even processing, compressed air is bubbled through the water. Later sodium hypochlorite is added to bleach the algae. Some sulfuric acid can be added to this mixture to regulate acidity.

2 hours
THE APPROXIMATE LENGTH OF TIME THE ALGAE IS COOKED

A World of Uses

Algae extracts are used in the manufacture of food products, medicines, cosmetics, medical supplies, and even tools. They can serve as emulsifying, stabilizing, thickening, or clarifying agents. Algae extracts are used in ice cream pie fillings, puddings, and salad dressings. They are also used for making molds in dentistry, for lubrication in drawing wire, and as a medium for culturing bacteria.

MILLING
The dry ground agar is milled to reduce particle size.

150 pounds
per square inch (10 kg/sq cm)
IS THE PRESSURE AT WHICH HOT AIR IS APPLIED TO DRY THE MASS.

CRUSHED ALGAE
Bleaching with salt water improves its quality.

GRINDING

MOIST GEL

DRYING BELT

GELLING

HOT AIR
160-175° F
(70-80° C)

PRESS

DRYING PRESS

QUALITY CONTROL
Samples are taken during successive stages of sifting.

GELATIN
contains 1% agar.

⑤

PRECAUTION
The dried algae must be ground immediately to prevent it from becoming moist.

Finishing

Ground into a powder, the product must go through successive milling and sifting steps to eliminate any lumps and impurities. Samples are taken as the algae product is refined. Once it has passed inspection, the final product is packaged.

GELLING
occurs when the temperature is lowered along the length of the pipe to 77° F (25° C).

④

Drying

Gel sheets about 0.4 inch (1 cm) wide come out of the press between layers of nylon. They are placed on platforms, where they begin to dry. The sheets are then placed on a conveyor belt and further dried by a stream of hot air.

③

Transformation

An initial filtering step uses only water and a filtering soil. The mixture must be kept in continuous motion and injected with steam to prevent it from separating. The mixture then passes through stainless steel pipes in which it is cooled to obtain a gelatin that contains 1 percent agar.

9 pounds
(4 kg)

THE QUANTITY OF FRESH ALGAE NEEDED TO OBTAIN ABOUT 2 POUNDS (1 KG) OF DRY ALGAE.

IN MEDICINE
Agar has laxative properties. Agar is also used as a medium for culturing microorganisms.

COLLOID
Algae extract is soluble only in hot water. It is used to add consistency to dairy products such as cheese, as well as to other food products.

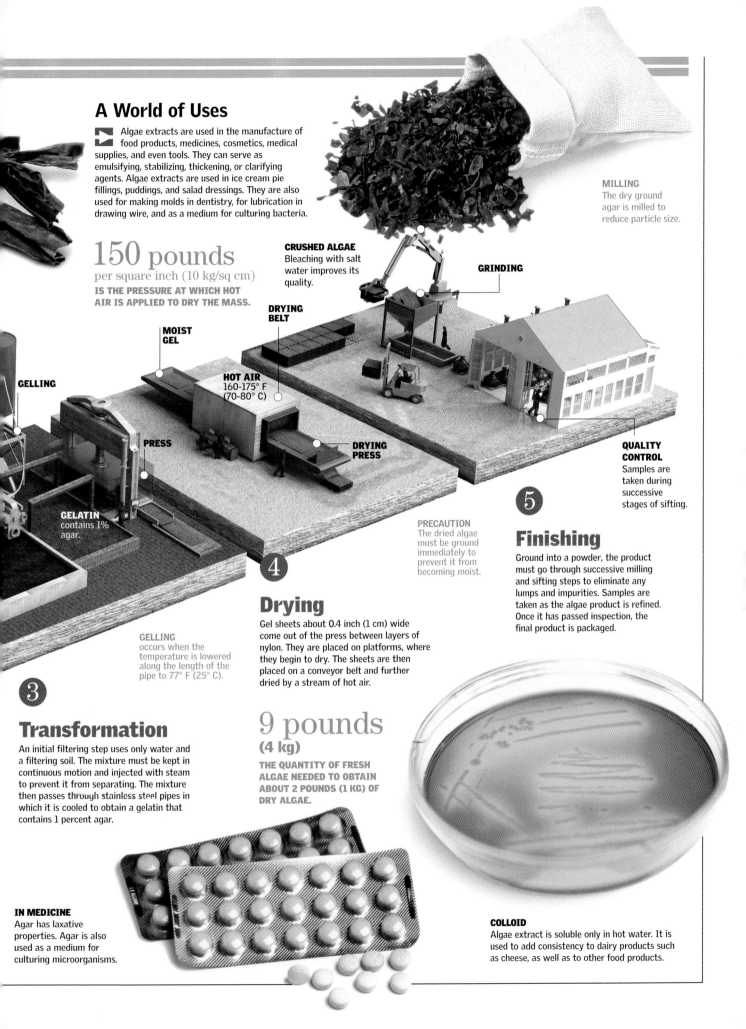

Strange Bedfellows

Lichens are the result of a close relationship between fungi and algae (usually green algae). Although they are most common in cold areas, they adapt easily to diverse climatic conditions. Lichens can grow in the Arctic glacial regions, as well as in deserts and volcanic regions. They live on rocks, from which they obtain all the necessary minerals to live, and they contribute to the formation of soils. Lichens are excellent indicators of the level of environmental pollution, since elevated levels of pollution cause them to die. ●

Fructicose

The long-branched thallus is raised or hanging and can resemble small trees or entangled bushes.

Pseudoevernia sp.

0.08 to 0.15 inch (2-4 mm)

IN THE MOUNTAINS
This lichen is common on the bark of mountain conifers. Its thallus looks like horns.

STIPES
The stipes are projections on the surface of the thallus at which vegetative multiplication takes place. Their shape is variable, and their color may be the same as or slightly darker than that of the thallus.

15,000
CLASSES OF LICHENS EXIST.

0.8 inch (2 cm)
THE AMOUNT A LICHEN CAN GROW IN A YEAR.

4,000 years
THE LIFE SPAN A LICHEN CAN ACHIEVE

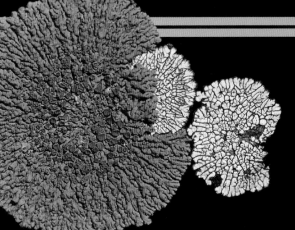

Crustaceans

With an appearance of scales, tightly affixed to the substratum, they can be continuous or fragmented in plates or areolas.

Physcia caesia

0.04 to 0.08 inch (1-2 mm)

Where They Live

Lichens grow in cold regions, as well as in the Amazon Rainforest and the desert. They are very sensitive to environmental pollution.

Corticolas
In trunks and branches

Terricolas
In the soil of forests

Saxicola
On rocks and walls.

A Symbiotic Relationship

Lichens are the result of symbiosis between a fungus and an alga, a relationship from which both benefit. In a lichen the fungus offers the alga support and moisture and protects it from heat and dehydration. Likewise, the alga produces food for itself and for the fungus through photosynthesis.

HOW IT IS CREATED

1 The spore of the fungus encounters the alga.

Hypha

Alga Cell

Germinating Spore

2 The spore grows around the alga, and the alga reproduces.

3 They form a new organism (thallus of the lichen).

Foliaceous

A showy lichen that has the appearance of widely spread leaves. It is the most common macrolichen.

Lobaria pulmonaria

0.1 to 0.2 inch (3-6 mm)

APOTHECIA
intervenes in the reproduction of the fungus because it contains its spores.

SOREDIA
Unit of lichen dispersion, formed by groups of gonidia surrounded by hyphae

HAIRS
Formed by the ends of the hyphae of the cortex or medulla

LAYER OF ALGAE
The layer contains green algae, which carry out photosynthesis to feed the fungus.

GONIDIA
Name given to algae when they form part of a lichen

LAYER OF FUNGI
The fungi are generally ascomycetes. They provide the alga with the moisture it needs to live.

HYPHAE
Fungal filaments, which are interwoven and colorless

MEDULLA
Made up of fungus hyphae

RICIN
Fixation organs that arise from the cortex or from the medulla

CORTEX
External layer of the lichen

Mosses

osses were among the earliest plants to emerge. They evolved from green algae more than 250 million years ago and belong to the group of simple plants called bryophytes. Mosses reproduce only in environments where liquid water is present. Because they grow in groups, they take on the appearance of a green carpet. These primitive plants can serve as indicators of air pollution, and they help reduce environmental degradation. ●

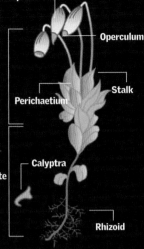

Capsule

Operculum

Sporophyte

Stalk

Perichaetium

Gametophyte

Calyptra

Rhizoid

DEVELOPMENT OF THE SPOROPHYTE
The zygote divides through mitosis and forms the sporophyte, which remains united to the gametophyte.

ADULT SPOROPHYTE
The adult sporophyte consists of a capsule (within which the spores form), a stalk (which holds the capsule), and a foot.

ZYGOTE
It forms from the union of two sexual cells in a watery environment.

Fertilization

Reproductive organs that produce gametes develop in the green gametophytes, which live all year long. When there is sufficient moisture, the male gamete reaches a female gamete and fertilizes it. The zygote that arises from this union grows and forms the sporophyte. The sporophyte possesses fertile tissue that undergoes meiosis to generate spores that, after falling to the ground and germinating, will form a new gametophyte.

DIPLOID
Diploid cells have two sets of chromosomes. Consequently, they have duplicate genetic information.

Spermatozoids

Archegonium:
the female sexual organ

Antheridium:
the male sexual organ

Ovule

HAPLOID
A haploid cell is one that contains only one complete set of genetic information. Reproductive cells, such as the ova and sperm in mammals, are haploid, but the rest of the cells in the body of higher organisms are usually diploid—that is, they have two complete sets of chromosomes. In fertilization two haploid gametes unite to form a diploid cell. In the case of mosses all the cells of the gametophyte, the gametes, and the spores are haploid.

ADULT GAMETOPHYTE
This is what a grown gametophyte looks like.

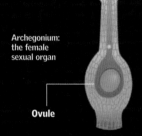

GERMINATION OF THE SPORE
The spore germinates and gives rise to a filamentous protonema (cellular mass).

GAMETOPHYTE DEVELOPMENT
The gametophyte grows.

HORIZONTAL FILAMENTS
The gametophyte develops from the horizontal filaments.

The Cycle of Life

Mosses do not have flowers, seeds, or fruits. As with other plants, mosses have a life cycle formed by alternating generations; however, in contrast with vascular plants, the haploid gametophyte is larger than the diploid sporophyte. Their biological cycle begins with the release of spores, which form in a capsule that opens when a small cap called the operculum is ejected. The spores germinate and give rise to a filamentous protonema (cellular mass) from which the gametophyte develops. The zygote that forms from the union of the two sexual cells develops into the sporophyte.

Rhizoids

Annulus

Operculum
A type of cap that covers the opening of the capsule and normally separates when the spores exit

Meiosis

Meiosis is a type of cellular division in which each daughter cell receives only one complete set of chromosomes. Therefore, the resulting cells have half as many chromosomes as the parent cells had. In general, this mechanism generates the gametes, but mosses generate haploid spores in the capsule of the sporophyte.

Mature Sporophyte
consists of a capsule in which spores are formed.

SPORES
The life cycle of a moss begins with the freeing of the spores that form in the capsule, which opens when a cap called the operculum is expulsed.

FUNARIA HIGROMETRICA
belongs to the group of plants called bryophytes.

10,000
SPECIES OF MOSSES
have been classified within the bryophite group of nonvascular plants.

Capsule
contains the spores and is found at the tip.

Small Plants

Mosses are bryophytes. They are relatively small plants that affix themselves to a substratum via rhizoids and carry out photosynthesis in small "leaves" that lack the specialized tissues of the real leaves of vascular plants. They fulfill a very important ecological role: they participate in the formation of soils by decomposing the rocks on which they grow, and they contribute to the photosynthesis of epiphytes in rainforests. Their asexual reproduction occurs through fragmentation or the production of propagula.

SPOROPHYTE
The sporophyte does not have an independent existence but lives at the expense of the gametophyte. The sporophyte lives a short time and only during a certain time of the year.

0.2 inch
(5 mm)

Dispersion of Spores

The fern is one of the oldest plants. Ferns have inhabited the surface of the Earth for 400 million years. Their leaves have structures called sori that contain the sporangium, which houses the spores. When the sori dry up, they release the spores into the air. Once on the ground, the spores germinate as gametophytes. In times of rain and abundant moisture the male cells of the gametophyte are able to swim to reach female gametes, which they fertilize to form a zygote that will grow as a sporophyte. ●

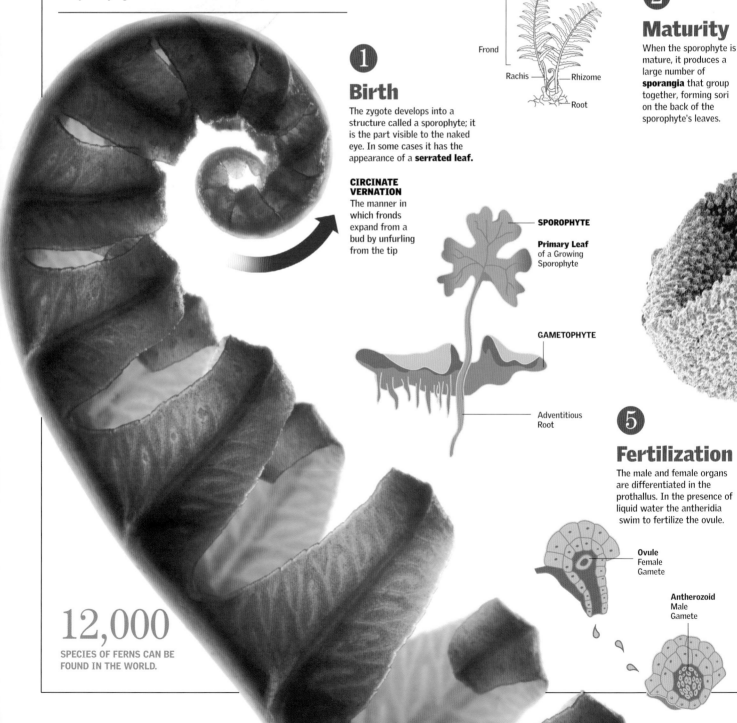

Pinnate

Frond

Rachis

Rhizome

Root

1 Birth

The zygote develops into a structure called a sporophyte; it is the part visible to the naked eye. In some cases it has the appearance of a **serrated leaf.**

CIRCINATE VERNATION
The manner in which fronds expand from a bud by unfurling from the tip

SPOROPHYTE

Primary Leaf of a Growing Sporophyte

GAMETOPHYTE

Adventitious Root

2 Maturity

When the sporophyte is mature, it produces a large number of **sporangia** that group together, forming sori on the back of the sporophyte's leaves.

5 Fertilization

The male and female organs are differentiated in the prothallus. In the presence of liquid water the antheridia swim to fertilize the ovule.

Ovule Female Gamete

Antherozoid Male Gamete

12,000
SPECIES OF FERNS CAN BE FOUND IN THE WORLD.

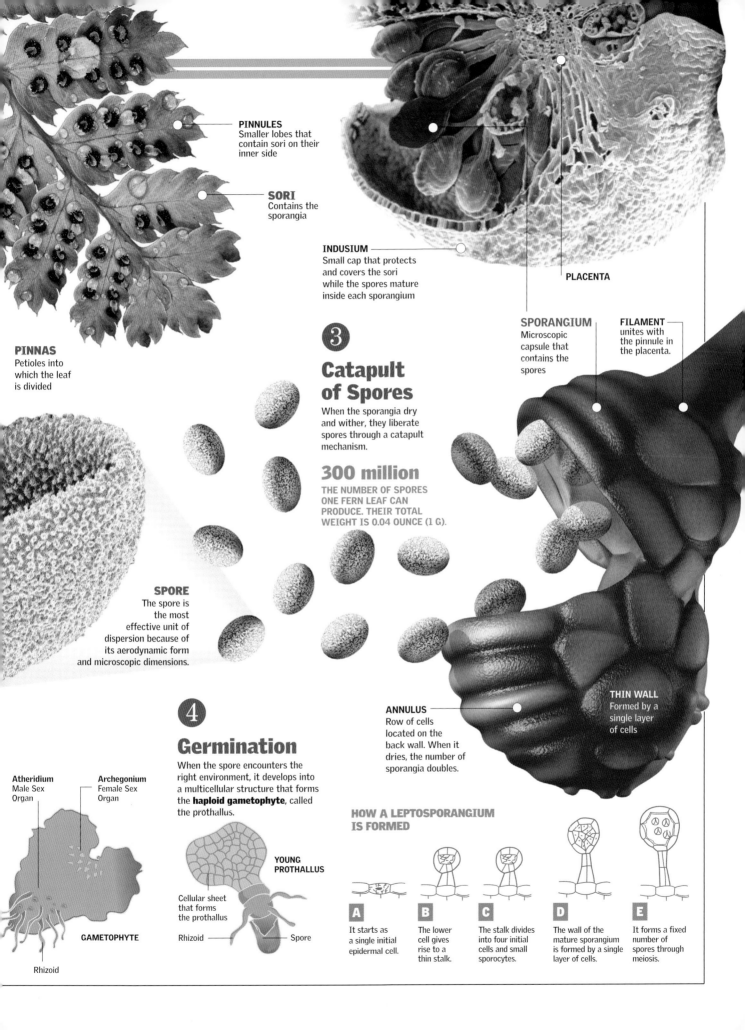

PINNULES
Smaller lobes that contain sori on their inner side

SORI
Contains the sporangia

INDUSIUM
Small cap that protects and covers the sori while the spores mature inside each sporangium

PLACENTA

PINNAS
Petioles into which the leaf is divided

SPORANGIUM
Microscopic capsule that contains the spores

FILAMENT
unites with the pinnule in the placenta.

③ Catapult of Spores

When the sporangia dry and wither, they liberate spores through a catapult mechanism.

300 million
THE NUMBER OF SPORES ONE FERN LEAF CAN PRODUCE. THEIR TOTAL WEIGHT IS 0.04 OUNCE (1 G).

SPORE
The spore is the most effective unit of dispersion because of its aerodynamic form and microscopic dimensions.

ANNULUS
Row of cells located on the back wall. When it dries, the number of sporangia doubles.

THIN WALL
Formed by a single layer of cells

④ Germination

When the spore encounters the right environment, it develops into a multicellular structure that forms the **haploid gametophyte**, called the prothallus.

Atheridium
Male Sex Organ

Archegonium
Female Sex Organ

GAMETOPHYTE

Rhizoid

YOUNG PROTHALLUS

Cellular sheet that forms the prothallus

Rhizoid — Spore

HOW A LEPTOSPORANGIUM IS FORMED

A It starts as a single initial epidermal cell.

B The lower cell gives rise to a thin stalk.

C The stalk divides into four initial cells and small sporocytes.

D The wall of the mature sporangium is formed by a single layer of cells.

E It forms a fixed number of spores through meiosis.

Seed Plants

nlike animals, plants are limited in their ability to seek favorable conditions for life and growth. Consequently, they have evolved in different ways to reproduce and increase their population through seeds. A seed must arrive at an appropriate location at the best time for germination. Each species achieves its objective in a

THE POLLEN REACHES THE STIGMA
This is the first step toward forming a seed. In this magnified image the grains of pollen can be seen on the stigma of wolfsbane (*Arnica montana*).

different way. Some produce a great number of seeds; others wrap their seeds in a layer of hard material that softens with rain and winter's cold to germinate in spring. In this chapter you will find how this process takes place, step by step, from pollination to the formation of a new plant.●

Seeds, To and Fro

Reproduction from seeds is the most prominent evolutionary advantage in plants' conquest of the terrestrial environment. The seed shelters the embryo of the future plant with protective walls. The embryo is accompanied by tissues that provide enough nutrients for it to begin to develop. Optimal temperature and an appropriate quantity of water and air are the factors that stimulate the seed to awaken to a marvelous cycle of development and growth that will culminate in the generation of new seeds. ●

1 Awakening of the Seed

Seeds, such as those of the field, or corn, poppy *(Papaver rhoeas)*, leave their latent stage when they hydrate and receive enough light and air. Their protective coverings open and the embryo grows thanks to the energy provided by its cotyledons, or seed leaves.

2 Tropism

Because of gravity, amyloplasts are always located in the lower part of cells. They produce a stimulus that encourages the root to grow toward the earth, a process called geotropism.

Cell multiplication allows the stem to grow.

PLUMULE
The bud of a plant embryo that will produce the first shoot

COTYLEDON
The first embryo leaf. It provides the energy needed for growth.

ABSORBENT HAIRS
These organs begin to develop in the radicle. They help the seed absorb water from the soil.

HARD COVER
Called the testa, it can appear in very different forms.

RADICLE
The embryo root that will produce the main root of the plant

Enzymes — Endosperm — Nutrients
Gibberellin — — Embryo
Seed Cover

The testa protects the embryo and the cotyledons during the seed's latent stage.

WATER
is responsible for breaking open seed covers because the hydrated tissues exert pressure on the interior of the seed.

NUTRIENTS
The radicle is in charge of collecting water and nutrients present in the soil.

Gibberellins

are plant hormones that, during the first stages of germination following water absorption, are distributed through the endosperm. Their presence promotes the production of enzymes that hydrolyze starches, lipids, and proteins to turn them into sugars, fatty acids, and amino acids, respectively. These substances provide nutrition to the embryo and later to the seedling.

Autum

THE TIME OF THE YEAR IN WHICH THE SEED OF *PAPAVER RHOEAS* GERMINATES

③ Growth

The seedling grows and breaks through the surface. This causes the plant to be exposed to light so it can begin to carry out photosynthesis. It thus begins to manufacture its own nutrients to replace those provided by the cotyledons.

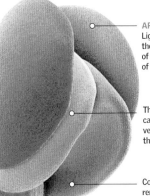

APICAL GROWTH
Light stimulates the multiplication of cells in the apex of the stem.

The cotyledon is carried by the vertical growth of the stem.

Cotyledons can remain under the soil or, as in this case, grow above the ground.

HYPOCOTYL
The first part of the stem that emerges and develops in the young plant

PRIMARY ROOT
It anchors itself to the ground and branches out to support the plant in the substrate.

④ Vegetative Growth

The first true leaves unfold above the cotyledons, and the stem elongates from formative tissue called the meristem, located at the apex of the plant. Continued growth will lead to the formation of an adult plant, which will develop its own reproductive structures.

TOTIPOTENCY
Characteristic of the vegetative apex cells

FIRST TRUE LEAVES

CONDUCTION
The stem carries water and minerals from the root to the leaves, while taking manufactured substances in the opposite direction.

0.4 inch (1 cm)
IS THE MAXIMUN HEIGHT IT CAN GROW IN ONE DAY.

SECONDARY ROOTS

FLOWERING
Internal and external changes stimulate the apical bud to develop a flower.

SESSILE LEAVES
The upper leaves have no petiole.

⑤ Production of the Flower's Parts

The apical bud begins to produce fertile flower structures (gynoecium and androecium) and sterile structures (petals and sepals). The flower bud forms.

ALTERNATE LEAVES

The root has many fine hairs that create a large surface area for water absorption.

THE FIRST 20 DAYS OF A FIELD POPPY

0.04 in (0.1 cm) | 3 in (8 cm) | 5 in (12 cm) | 6 in (15 cm) | 8 in (20 cm)

20 inches (50 cm)
THE TYPICAL HEIGHT OF AN ADULT FIELD POPPY PLANT

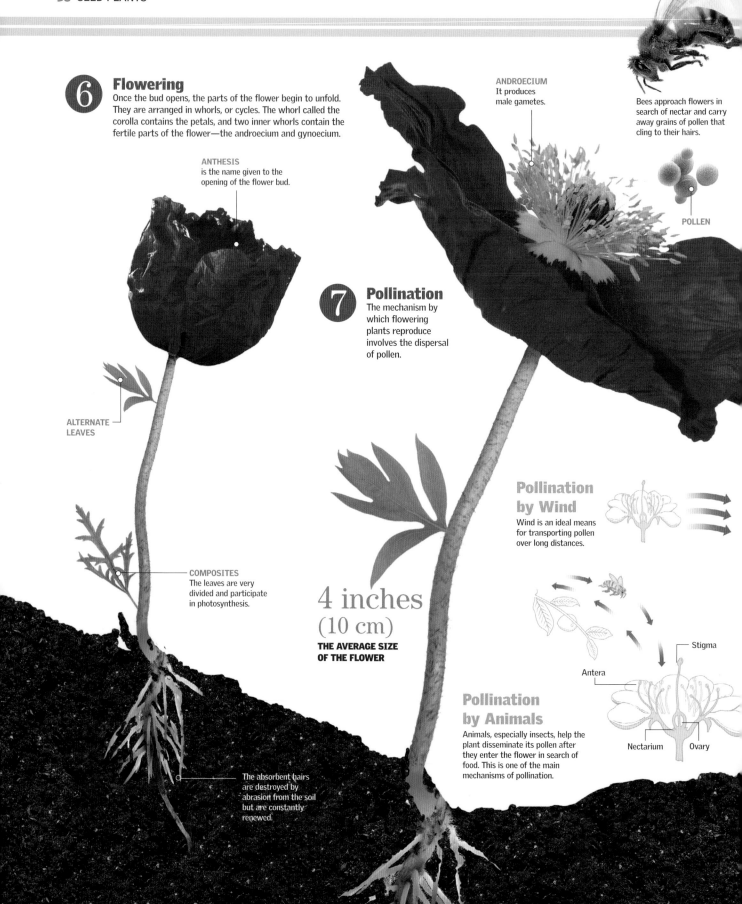

6 Flowering

Once the bud opens, the parts of the flower begin to unfold. They are arranged in whorls, or cycles. The whorl called the corolla contains the petals, and two inner whorls contain the fertile parts of the flower—the androecium and gynoecium.

ANTHESIS
is the name given to the opening of the flower bud.

ALTERNATE LEAVES

COMPOSITES
The leaves are very divided and participate in photosynthesis.

The absorbent hairs are destroyed by abrasion from the soil but are constantly renewed.

ANDROECIUM
It produces male gametes.

Bees approach flowers in search of nectar and carry away grains of pollen that cling to their hairs.

POLLEN

7 Pollination

The mechanism by which flowering plants reproduce involves the dispersal of pollen.

**4 inches
(10 cm)**
**THE AVERAGE SIZE
OF THE FLOWER**

Pollination by Wind

Wind is an ideal means for transporting pollen over long distances.

Pollination by Animals

Animals, especially insects, help the plant disseminate its pollen after they enter the flower in search of food. This is one of the main mechanisms of pollination.

Stigma

Antera

Nectarium   Ovary

FRUIT
After fertilization the ovary and adjacent tissues become the fruit.

STAMENS

FRUIT

SEEDS

8 Fruit

The seeds develop inside the fruit. Each seed can develop a new seedling.

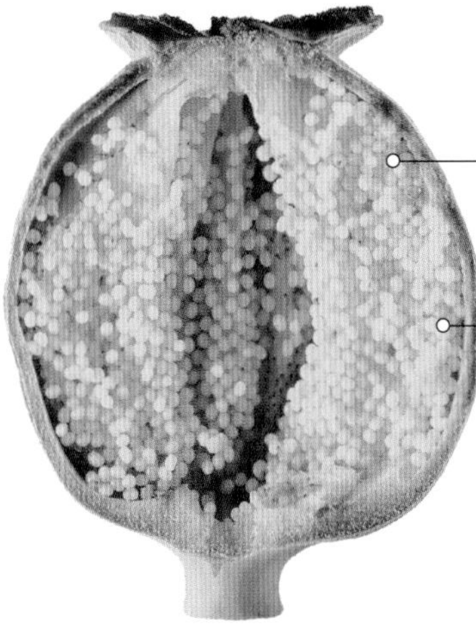

9 Ripe Fruit

The fruits scatter the seeds. Field poppies have dry fruits that open when they mature. This facilitates the dispersion of the seed by air.

SEMILLAS

10 Dispersion

The fruit of a field poppy is a capsule with small openings at the top that help scatter the seeds.

11 Seed

Each seed distributed by air, water, or an animal can, under the right environmental conditions, germinate and develop into a new seedling.

3,000

SEEDS CAN BE CONTAINED IN ONE RIPE FIELD POPPY FRUIT.

Something in Common

When a seed encounters the right conditions, it can begin its life cycle. Even though every species of plant with flowers has its own particular life cycle, the various stages of the cycle represented here are typical of angiosperms in general.

Under the Earth

The root is a plant organ that is usually found under the soil. It has positive geotropism; its main functions are absorbing water and inorganic nutrients and attaching the plant to the ground. The root is essential for identifying the particular characteristics of a plant. The anatomical structure of a root can vary, but, because it does not have leaves or nodes, it will always be simpler than that of a stem.

Types of Roots

Roots differ, depending on their origin. The primary root originates in the radicle of the embryo. An adventitious root is one that originates in any other organ of the plant. Roots are also subdivided according to their morphology.

TAPROOT
A taproot grows downward and has lateral secondary roots that are not well developed.

FIBROUS
The root system is formed by a group of roots of similar diameter.

NAPIFORM
The taproot thickens with stored food and tapers abruptly near its tip.

BRANCHED
The main root is divided, creating other secondary roots.

TUBEROUS
Fibrous in structure, some of the roots thicken to store food for the plant.

TABULAR
Tabular roots form at the base of a trunk and create a supporting buttress.

GEOTROPISM
Geotropism, or gravitotropism, is the growth of a plant or parts of a plant in a particular direction because of the stimulus of gravity. The force of gravity orients the stems and their leaves to grow upward (negative geotropism), whereas the roots grow downward (positive geotropism).

Monocotyledons
These plants have embryos with only one cotyledon. Their embryonic root generally has a relatively short life and is replaced by adventitious roots that grow from the stem.

GROWTH AND CELLULAR DIVISION
Through the process of cell division a cell divides into two cells, each with its own nucleus. The new cells elongate, allowing the root to grow in thickness and length.

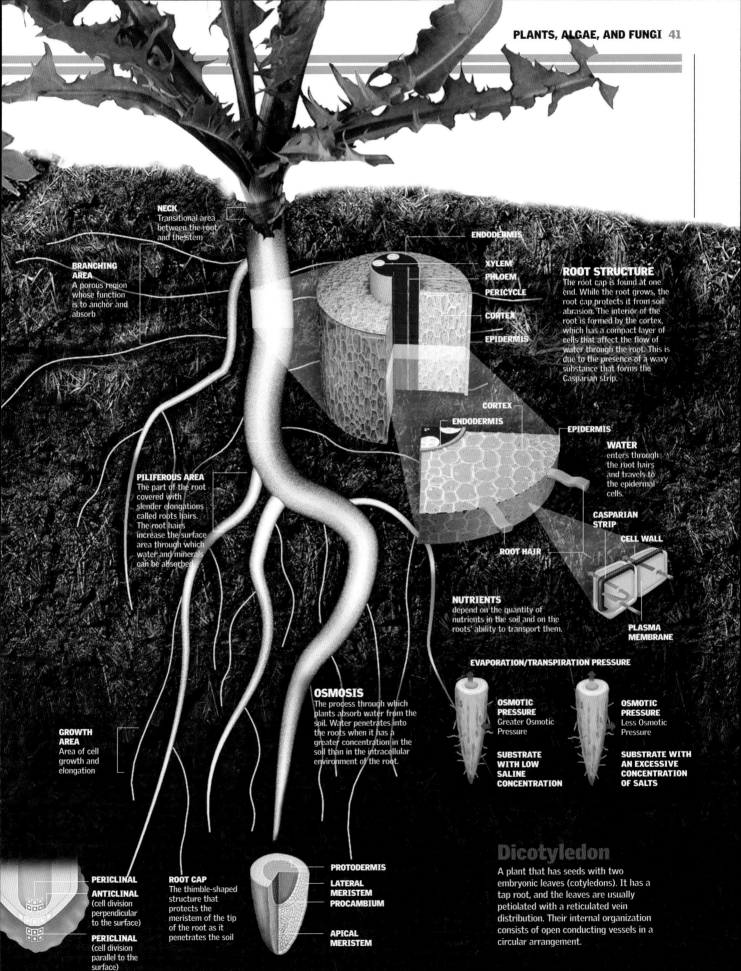

NECK
Transitional area between the root and the stem

BRANCHING AREA
A porous region whose function is to anchor and absorb

ENDODERMIS

XYLEM

PHLOEM

PERICYCLE

CORTEX

EPIDERMIS

ROOT STRUCTURE
The root cap is found at one end. While the root grows, the root cap protects it from soil abrasion. The interior of the root is formed by the cortex, which has a compact layer of cells that affect the flow of water through the root. This is due to the presence of a waxy substance that forms the Casparian strip.

CORTEX

ENDODERMIS

EPIDERMIS

WATER
enters through the root hairs and travels to the epidermal cells.

PILIFEROUS AREA
The part of the root covered with slender elongations called roots hairs. The root hairs increase the surface area through which water and minerals can be absorbed.

CASPARIAN STRIP

CELL WALL

ROOT HAIR

NUTRIENTS
depend on the quantity of nutrients in the soil and on the roots' ability to transport them.

PLASMA MEMBRANE

EVAPORATION/TRANSPIRATION PRESSURE

OSMOSIS
The process through which plants absorb water from the soil. Water penetrates into the roots when it has a greater concentration in the soil than in the intracellular environment of the root.

OSMOTIC PRESSURE
Greater Osmotic Pressure

SUBSTRATE WITH LOW SALINE CONCENTRATION

OSMOTIC PRESSURE
Less Osmotic Pressure

SUBSTRATE WITH AN EXCESSIVE CONCENTRATION OF SALTS

GROWTH AREA
Area of cell growth and elongation

PERICLINAL

ANTICLINAL
(cell division perpendicular to the surface)

PERICLINAL
(cell division parallel to the surface)

ROOT CAP
The thimble-shaped structure that protects the meristem of the tip of the root as it penetrates the soil

PROTODERMIS

LATERAL MERISTEM

PROCAMBIUM

APICAL MERISTEM

Dicotyledon

A plant that has seeds with two embryonic leaves (cotyledons). It has a tap root, and the leaves are usually petiolated with a reticulated vein distribution. Their internal organization consists of open conducting vessels in a circular arrangement.

Stems: More Than a Support

Stems, which occur in a variety of shapes and colors, support a plant's leaves and flowers. They keep it from breaking apart in the wind, and they determine its height. In addition, stems are also responsible for distributing the water and minerals absorbed by a plant's roots. Stems contain conducting vessels through which water and nutrients circulate. In trees and bushes, stems are woody for better support. ●

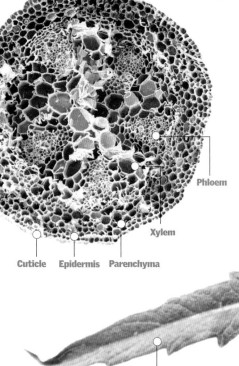

CROSS-SECTION OF A NEW STEM

Phloem

Xylem

Cuticle   Epidermis   Parenchyma

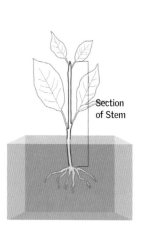

Section of Stem

IN THE AIR
Stems are usually branched, as seen in trees and bushes.

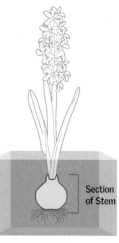

Section of Stem

IN THE GROUND
Certain types of stems have unusual characteristics.

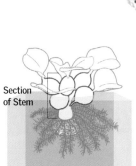

Section of Stem

IN THE WATER
The stem of an aquatic plant can lie underwater.

LEAF

Development of Stems in Different Mediums

Stems have widely varying sizes and shapes that reflect different adaptations to the environment. Palm trees and wheat are two good examples that show how different mediums can modify the stem through evolution. Palm trees are the tallest non-woody plants. They grow tall because they must compete with many other plants for sunlight. In contrast, wheat is typical of areas with a cold climate and a short growing season. It develops a relatively short stem. This enables it to survive the physical assault of the dry wind and the loss of leaves.

SPROUTS
grow from the eyes.

COMMON POTATO
Solanum tuberosum

TUBER
An underground stem composed mainly of parenchymatic cells filled with starch. The potato's small depressions are actually axillary eyes. In an onion, another example of a plant with an underground stem, starch accumulates not in tubers but in thick leaves that grow around the stem.

AXILLARY EYES
are grouped in a spiral pattern along the potato.

ARTICHOKE THISTLE
Cynara cardunculus

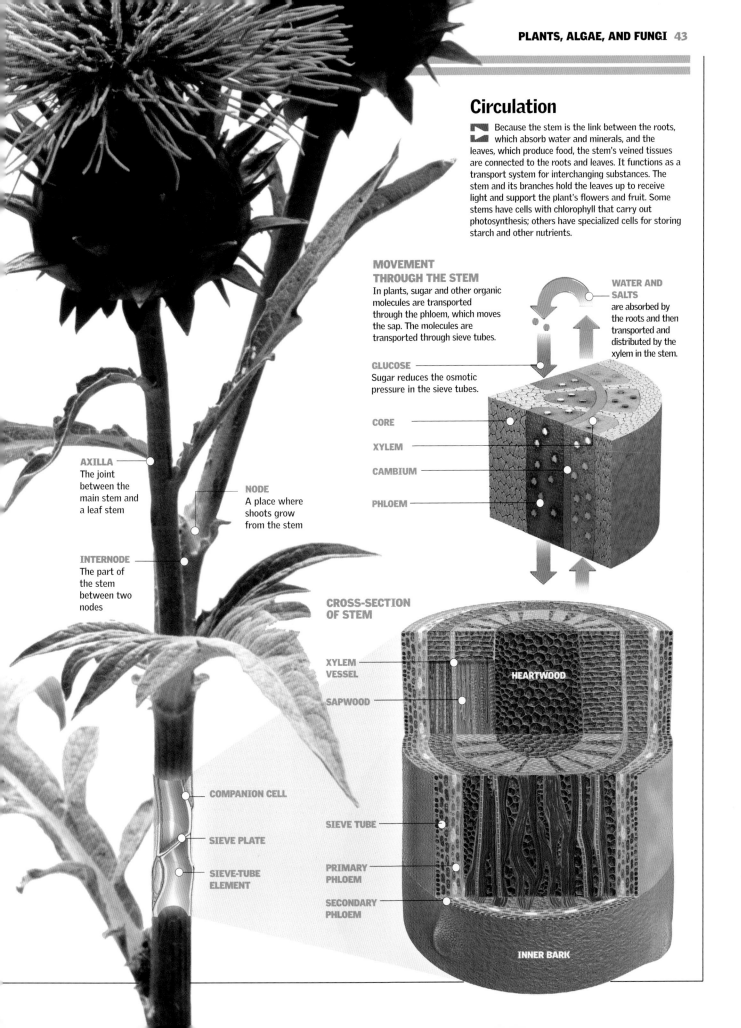

Circulation

Because the stem is the link between the roots, which absorb water and minerals, and the leaves, which produce food, the stem's veined tissues are connected to the roots and leaves. It functions as a transport system for interchanging substances. The stem and its branches hold the leaves up to receive light and support the plant's flowers and fruit. Some stems have cells with chlorophyll that carry out photosynthesis; others have specialized cells for storing starch and other nutrients.

MOVEMENT THROUGH THE STEM

In plants, sugar and other organic molecules are transported through the phloem, which moves the sap. The molecules are transported through sieve tubes.

WATER AND SALTS
are absorbed by the roots and then transported and distributed by the xylem in the stem.

GLUCOSE
Sugar reduces the osmotic pressure in the sieve tubes.

CORE

XYLEM

CAMBIUM

PHLOEM

AXILLA
The joint between the main stem and a leaf stem

NODE
A place where shoots grow from the stem

INTERNODE
The part of the stem between two nodes

CROSS-SECTION OF STEM

XYLEM VESSEL

SAPWOOD

HEARTWOOD

COMPANION CELL

SIEVE PLATE

SIEVE-TUBE ELEMENT

SIEVE TUBE

PRIMARY PHLOEM

SECONDARY PHLOEM

INNER BARK

Wooden Heart

Every year a tree thickens its trunk through the production of growth rings, a process called secondary growth. Each new ring is different from the ring that grew the year before. This happens because the wood produced over the course of a year varies in its composition and in the time it takes to form a ring. Trees are the largest producers of wood, which can be processed as hand-cut wood, logs, or sawed lumber—the most common form in the industry. To calculate a tree's age scientists study its growth rings. ●

1 Initiation
The layer of meristematic cells formed between the xylem and the phloem develops inside the base tissue until it grows all the way around, forming a cylinder.

- Epidermis
- Cortex
- Primary Phloem
- Primary Xylem

Secondary Growth

Secondary growth takes place in the secondary meristems: the vascular cambium and the cork cambium. The vascular cambium is found between the xylem and the phloem at the end of the plant's primary growth zone. It produces secondary xylem toward the inside of the trunk and secondary phloem toward the outside.

2 Lengthening
The primary xylem and phloem form when the vascular cambium divides.

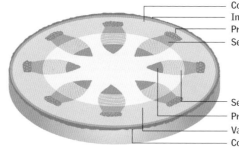

- Cortical Parenchyma
- Inner Bark
- Primary Phloem
- Secondary Phloem
- Secondary Xylem
- Primary Xylem
- Vascular Cambium
- Cork Cambium

A Tree's Age

Dendrochronology is the study of the age of trees. The number of growth rings formed since a tree's birth establishes its age.

LABURNUM
Laburmun sp.

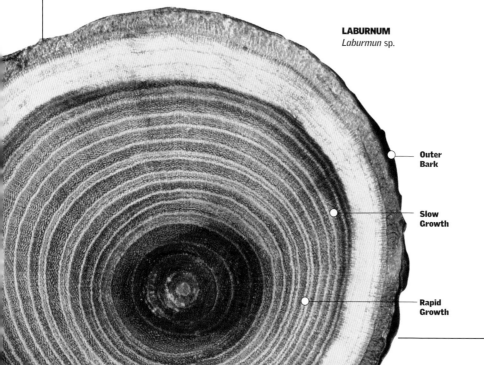

- Primary Xylem
- Secondary Xylem
- Primary Phloem
- Secondary Phloem
- Cortical Parenchyma
- Vascular Cambium
- Cork Cambium

- **Outer Bark**
- **Slow Growth**
- **Rapid Growth**

SPECIES
Most of the 70,000 known tree species are dicotyledons. However, the oldest trees (4,900-year-old bristlecone pines [*Pinus longaeva*]) and the tallest trees (360 foot [110 m] sequoias [*Sequoia sempervirens*]) are gymnosperms. The earliest trees known to paleobotany appeared during the Devonian Period.

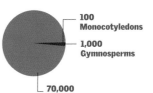

100 Monocotyledons

1,000 Gymnosperms

70,000 Dicotyledons

PHLOEM
The phloem transports the products of photosynthesis, mostly in the form of sucrose. This is its main function.

INNER BARK
is the youngest ring, because a new ring is created in each year's growth.

TYPES OF WOOD
Wood comes from two main groups of trees:

Wood in angiosperms is the product of the activity of the cambium and the environmental conditions that exist during the wood's formation.

The wood of conifers (gymnosperms) tends to be simpler and more uniform than that of angiosperms. The woody tissue consists mainly of tracheids.

3 Termination
The veined cambium forms the primary and secondary vein tissues.

XYLEM
Its main function is to carry water and mineral salts from the roots to the leaves.

SAPWOOD
is the woody part of the trunk and consists of xylem tissue. It is pale in color and of variable thickness.

Rolled Logs
Not processed before use, they are often used in rural and traditional construction.

Hand-Hewn Wood
is chopped by hand with an ax. It is used in rural construction for rafters and posts, but it involves a considerable loss of wood.

Sawed Lumber
It is cut to specified dimensions, either manually or mechanically, in a sawmill. It is the type of wood most often used in construction.

Growth Springs Eternal

Some vascular (veined) plants, also called tracheophytes, are able to continue growing year after year. This is made possible by meristems, groups of stem cells that retain the ability to divide. There are two types of meristems: apical, which carry on the plant's primary growth, and lateral, which give rise to the tissues that increase the plant's girth. As the meristematic cells form new cells, the plant grows and renews its organs. Thanks to their growth buds, the plants maintain their vitality and strengthen their organs or replace them often. Because of this process, the renewed plants are able to increase their number of branches, flowers, and leaves. ●

Without Bracts
Some buds, such as those in plants of the cabbage family (Brassicaceae), are not covered by bracts. Instead, the vegetable's growth zone is covered by outer leaves.

INFRAPETIOLAR BUD
The axillary bud is joined to the petiole of a leaf. The growth of the leaf carries the bud outward. This often occurs in plants with inflorescences, or flowers that grow on branches.

SUPERPOSED BUD
The axillary bud is joined to the stem. As the cells of the internode multiply, they carry the axillary bud, which then appears to be inserted above the leaf.

Branching

Growth buds can be found at the end of the main axis (apical bud) or at the joint where the leaves meet the stem (lateral bud). Growth can take different forms, depending on the type of bud that predominates. If apical buds are more common, the branch growth is called monopodial. If lateral buds predominate, the branch growth is called sympodial. Conifers are an example of monopodial growth. Sympodial growth is widespread among dicotyledon herbs and is found in practically all monocotyledons.

PHYLLOTAXIS
is the name of the order of plants whose leaves are arranged along the nodes of the branches. Each node can have from one to several leaves.

SYCAMORE MAPLE
Acer pseudoplatanus

ALTERNATING
One leaf per node, arranged alternately in successive nodes. Found in monocots and dicots.

Stem | Arrangement of Leaves

GIANT SEA HOLLY
Eryngium giganteum

VERTICILATE
Several leaves per node. Whorls are formed in a spiral arrangement around successive nodes.

Stem | Arrangement of Leaves

GUM ROCKROSE
Citus ladanifer

OPPOSITE
Two leaves per node. They are arranged perpendicularly to earlier and later nodes.

Stem | Arrangement of Leaves

CLARY SAGE
Salvia sclarea

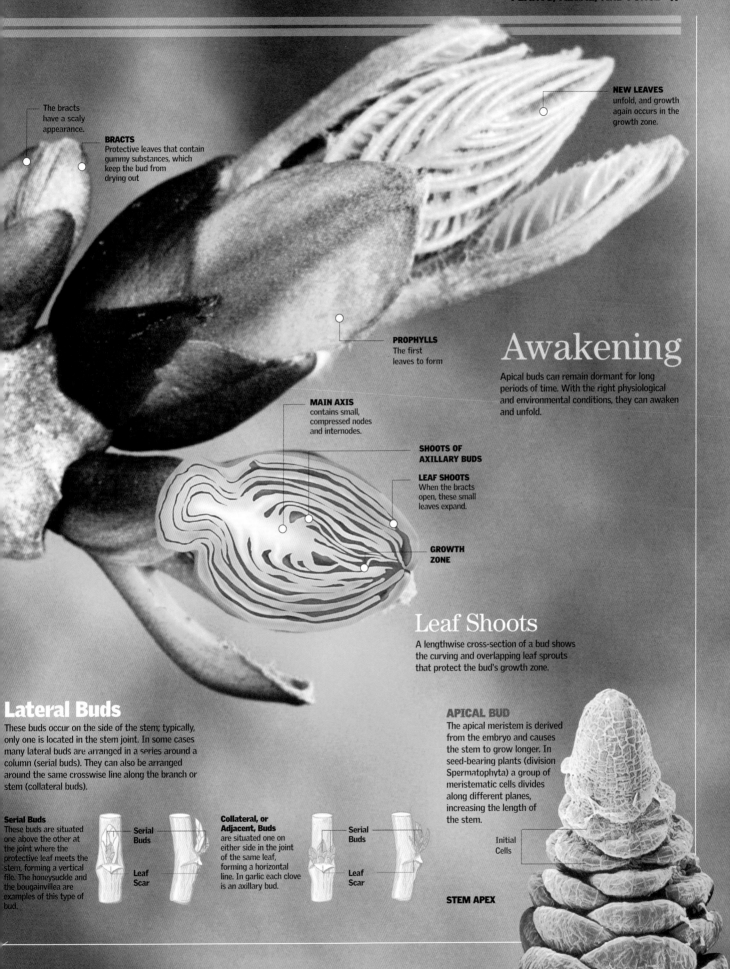

- The bracts have a scaly appearance.

BRACTS
Protective leaves that contain gummy substances, which keep the bud from drying out

NEW LEAVES
unfold, and growth again occurs in the growth zone.

PROPHYLLS
The first leaves to form

MAIN AXIS
contains small, compressed nodes and internodes.

SHOOTS OF AXILLARY BUDS

LEAF SHOOTS
When the bracts open, these small leaves expand.

GROWTH ZONE

Awakening

Apical buds can remain dormant for long periods of time. With the right physiological and environmental conditions, they can awaken and unfold.

Leaf Shoots

A lengthwise cross-section of a bud shows the curving and overlapping leaf sprouts that protect the bud's growth zone.

Lateral Buds

These buds occur on the side of the stem; typically, only one is located in the stem joint. In some cases many lateral buds are arranged in a series around a column (serial buds). They can also be arranged around the same crosswise line along the branch or stem (collateral buds).

Serial Buds
These buds are situated one above the other at the joint where the protective leaf meets the stem, forming a vertical file. The honeysuckle and the bougainvillea are examples of this type of bud.

Serial Buds

Leaf Scar

Collateral, or Adjacent, Buds
are situated one on either side in the joint of the same leaf, forming a horizontal line. In garlic each clove is an axillary bud.

Serial Buds

Leaf Scar

APICAL BUD
The apical meristem is derived from the embryo and causes the stem to grow longer. In seed-bearing plants (division Spermatophyta) a group of meristematic cells divides along different planes, increasing the length of the stem.

Initial Cells

STEM APEX

Energy Manufacturers

The main function of leaves is to carry out photosynthesis. Their shape is specialized to capture light energy and transform it into chemical energy. Their thinness minimizes their volume and maximizes their surface area that is exposed to the Sun. However, there are a great many variations on this basic theme, which have evolved in association with different types of weather conditions. ●

EDGES (MARGINS)
Species are distinguished by a wide variety of edges: smooth, jagged, and wavy.

PRIMARY VEINS
The products of photosynthesis circulate through the veins from the leaves to the rest of the body.

VEINS
Flowering plants (division Angiosperma) are often distinguished by the type of veins they have: parallel veins in monocots and branching veins in dicots.

RACHIS

ACER SP.
This genus includes trees and bushes easily distinguishable by their opposite and lobed leaves.

LEAF STEM (PETIOLE)

LEAF SURFACE
Colorful, usually green, with darker shades on the upper, or adaxial, side. The veins can be readily seen.

Simple Leaves
In most monocotyledon plants the leaf is undivided. In some cases it may have lobes or notches in its side, but these divisions do not reach all the way to the primary vein of the leaf.

Compound Leaves
When the leaf is divided from the primary vein, it forms separate leaflets. A compound leaf is called palmate when the leaflets are arranged like the fingers on a hand and pinnate when they grow from the sides of the leaf stem like the barbs of a feather.

CROSS-SECTION

In general, upon sectioning a leaf, one can observe that it possesses the same tissues as the rest of the body of the plant. The distribution of tissues varies with each species.

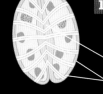

1 The stomatic apparatus is closed. No air can enter or leave the leaf. This prevents excessive transpiration, which could damage the plant.

Thickened cell walls in the area of the pore

Cellulose Microfibers

CONDUCTING TISSUE

is made of live cells (phloem) and dead cells (xylem).

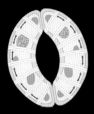

2 The stomatic apparatus is open. The stomatic cells are swollen. As tension increases, the cellular form is modified and is able to exchange gases.

PLANTS AND THE ENVIRONMENT

The flow of carbon dioxide and water vapor between the plant and the environment is essential for the photosynthetic process. This exchange can be affected by internal or external factors, such as changes in light, temperature, or humidity. In response to these stimuli the stomas can open or close.

BASIC TISSUE

is formed by live cells that give structure to the leaf and usually contain some chloroplasts.

EPIDERMAL TISSUE

is composed of live cells. It surrounds all the parts of the leaf and the plant. It produces a substance that forms the cuticle.

Change and Its Advantages

Conifers possess an interesting modification in their leaves. In these gymnosperms evolution directed the abrupt reduction of surface foliage area. This gave them an adaptive advantage over plants whose leaves have a large surface area: less resistance to wind and less transpiration in arid climates. In addition, they are able to avoid the excessive weight that would result from the accumulation of snow on large leaves.

TENDRILS

The leaves of climbing plants, such as the grapevine, have these adaptive modifications.

VASCULAR BUNDLE
Formed by phloem and xylem

RESIN
functions to prevent freezing. It circulates through the resin ducts.

EPIDERMIS
Cells with thick walls and a thick cuticle

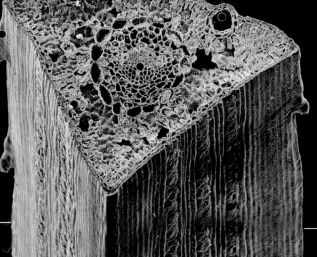

CONIFERS

Needle-shaped leaves are characteristic of conifers. They are usually oval or triangular. A hypodermis, which is enclosed by the epidermis, is broken only in the stomas.

Functional Beauty

Flowers are not simply beautiful objects; they are also the place where the reproductive organs of angiosperms are located. Many are hermaphroditic, meaning that they contain both the male reproductive apparatus (the androecium) and the female (the gynoecium). The process of pollination is carried out through external agents, such as insects, birds, wind, and water. Following fertilization, flowers produce seeds in their ovaries. The floral parts are arranged in circular or spiral patterns. ●

Gynoecium
The female reproductive system. It is formed by carpels and includes the ovary, ovules, style, and stigma.

STIGMA
It can be simple or divided. It secretes a sticky liquid that captures the pollen. Some are also covered with hair.

Classification

Plants with flowers are classified as dicotyledons or monocotyledons. The first group has seeds with two cotyledons, and the second has seeds with only one. Each represents a different evolutionary line. They are differentiated by the structure of their organs. The cotyledon contains nutrients that the embryo utilizes during its growth until its true leaves appear. When a seed germinates, the first thing that appears is the root. In monocotyledons the stem and the radicle are protected by a membrane; the dicotyledons lack this protection, and the stem pushes itself through the soil.

Dicotyledons

In this class of plants each whorl of the flower is arranged in groups of four or five parts. In dicotyledons the sepal is small and green, the petals are large and colorful, and the leaves are wide. The vascular ducts are cylindrical.

FLORAL DIAGRAM

OVARY
The ovary is found in the receptacle at the base of the gynoecium, inside the carpels. The pollen tube extends into the ovary and penetrates the ovule.

LEAVES
In dicotyledons, leaves have various forms, and they contain a network of veins that connect with a primary vein.

Monocotyledons

Each whorl of these flowers contains three parts, and their sepals and petals are generally not differentiated from one another. The majority are herbaceous plants with scattered vascular conduits. They are the most evolved species of angiosperms.

FLORAL DIAGRAM

CARPEL
The carpel consists of modified leaves that together form the gynoecium. It contains a stigma, a style, and an ovary. Ovules are produced in the ovary.

LEAVES
Plants with only one cotyledon have large and narrow leaves, with parallel veins and no petiole.

ROOT
In dicotyledons the main root penetrates the ground vertically as a prolongation of the stem, and secondary roots extend from it horizontally. It can be very deep and long-lived.

Androecium

The male reproductive system. It is formed by a group of stamens, each of which consists of an anther supported by a filament. The base may contain glands that produce nectar.

ANTHER
A sac where grains of pollen (the male gametes) are produced

FILAMENT
Its function is to sustain the anther.

Whorls

Most flowers have four whorls. In a typical flower the outermost whorl is the calyx, followed by the corolla, the androecium (which can have two parts), and the gynoecium. When a flower has all four whorls, it is considered complete; it is incomplete when it lacks at least one of them. Plants that have an androecium and a gynoecium, but in separate flowers, are called monoecious. If the flower lacks a sepal and petals, it is said to be naked.

250,000

THE NUMBER OF KNOWN SPECIES OF ANGIOSPERM PLANTS, THOUGH ONLY 1,000 SPECIES HAVE ECONOMIC IMPORTANCE. ABOUT TWO THIRDS OF THESE SPECIES ARE NATIVE TO THE TROPICS.

COROLLA
A grouping of petals. If its parts are separated, they are simply called petals; if they are united, the plant is described as gamopetalous.

PETAL
It typically has a showy color to attract pollinating insects or other animals.

STYLE
Some styles are solid, others hollow. Their number depends on the number of carpels. The pollen tube grows through the style. In corn the tube can reach a length of 15 inches (40 cm).

CALYX
The grouping of sepals that protects the other parts of the flower. Together with the corolla it forms the perianth. The sepals may be separate or united; in the latter case the plant is called gamosepalous.

SEPAL
Each of the modified leaves that protect the flower in its first stage of development. They also prevent insects from gaining access to the nectar without completing their pollinating function. Sepals are usually green.

OVARY
The ovary is found in the receptacle in the base of the gynoecium, inside the carpels. The pollen tube, which conducts the pollen to the ovule, extends to the ovary.

TEPAL
In monocotyledonous plants the petals and sepals are usually the same. In this case they are called tepals, and the group of tepals is called a perianth.

ROOT
In monocotyledons all the roots branch from the same point, forming a kind of dense hair. They are generally superficial and short-lived.

Pollination

The orchid, whose scientific name *Ophrys apifera* means "bee orchid," is so called because of the similarity between the texture of its flowers and the body of a bee. Orchids' flowers are large and very colorful, and they secrete a sugary nectar that is eaten by many insects. The orchid is an example of a zoomophilous species; this means that its survival is based on attracting birds or insects that will transport its pollen to distant flowers and fertilize them.

CAUDICLE
At times it closes, covering the pollinia.

ODOR
The odor is similar to bee pheromones.

POLLINIUM
A small clump of closely packed pollen grains

1
Attraction

When a flower opens, a liquid drips on its lower petal and forms a small pool. The liquid gives off an intense aroma that attracts bees.

POLLINATING INSECT
Male Bee
Gorytes sp.

3
The Load

While passing through the narrow tunnel, the bee brushes the pollinarium, and pollen sticks to the bee.

2
The Fall

Excited by the perfume and the texture, the bee enters the flower, and in this pseudo-copulation it usually falls into the pool and becomes trapped. It cannot fly and can only escape by climbing the flower's stamens.

NECTAR
A sugary liquid that is somewhat sticky

Bee Orchid
Ophyrys apifera

LABELLUM
Its form imitates the abdomen of the bee.

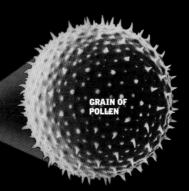

POLLINIA
Small clumps of pollen grains housed in a compartment of the anther

0.008 to 0.08 inch (0.2-2 mm)

POLLINARIUM
Grouping of two, four, six, or eight pollinia

GRAIN OF POLLEN

Pollen
Each grain contains a male gamete.

12,000
THE NUMBER OF SEEDS THAT A SINGLE FERTILIZED ORCHID PRODUCES

CORBICULUM
Organ for the transport of pollen

COLORATION
is one of the factors of attraction.

4
Transfer
The bee takes off toward other flowers, with pollen from the orchid stuck to its back.

LOBULES
They have fine, silky hairs that attract the bees.

5
Toward a Destination
When it arrives at another flower of the same species, the bee repeats the incursion and bumps the flower's stigmas (female organs), depositing pollen that is capable of fertilizing it.

CAMOUFLAGE
Some plants that rely on insects for pollination acquire the appearance of the animal species on which they depend for survival. Each orchid has its own pollinating insect.

Bearing Fruit

O nce the flower is fertilized, its ovary matures and develops, first to protect the seed forming within it and then to disperse the seed. The stigmas and anthers wither, and the ovary transforms into fruit. Its wall forms the cover, or pericarp. Fruits and seeds are of great economic importance because of their key role in human nutrition. The endosperms of some seeds are rich in starch, proteins, fats, and oils. ●

Simple Fruits

come from a single flower. They may contain one or more seeds and be dry or fleshy. Among them are drupes, berries, and pomes.

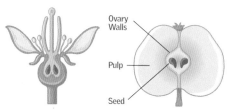

Ovary Walls
Pulp
Seed

A POMES
are fleshy fruits that come from epigynous flowers, or flowers whose enclosed ovaries lie below the place where the other parts of the flower are attached. The floral receptacle thickens and forms an edible mesicarp. Apples are one example.

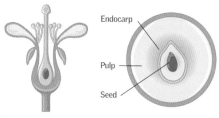

Endocarp
Pulp
Seed

B DRUPES
are fleshy fruits, leathery or fibrous, which are surrounded by a woody endocarp with a seed in its interior. They are generally derived from hypogynous flowers—flowers whose ovaries lie above the point where the other flower parts are attached. An example is the peach.

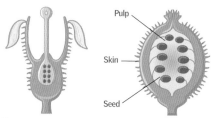

Pulp
Skin
Seed

C BERRIES
When they mature, berries generally have a bright color and a fleshy or juicy mesocarp. They come from either epigynous or hypogynous flowers. The grape is an example.

Oranges

Like other citrus fruits, oranges are similar to berries. Their seeds may propagate when the fruit rots and exposes them or when an animal eats the fruit and then defecates the seeds.

Seeds

Loculos

Central Axis

Septos

Vesicles

ENDOCARP
The part of the pericarp that contains the seeds. It is formed in parts, or sections.

MESOCARP
A fleshy structure that is relatively solid

14%

THE PROPORTION OF AN IMMATURE CITRUS FRUIT THAT IS MADE UP OF THE FLAVONOID GLYCOSIDE (HESPERIDIN)

Section

A sac that fills with juices (reserves of water and sugar) produced by the ovary walls

Peel

It consists of the mesocarp and exocarp of the fruit. It is soft and secretes oils and acids. However, in the case of a nut, its hard "peel" is its endocarp.

Multiple Fruits

are those that develop from the carpels of more than one flower, in a condensed inflorescence. When they mature, they are fleshy. An example is the fig.

BLACKBERRY
In this aggregate fruit, each berry is a fruit.

FIG
Condensed fruit

A AGGREGATE FRUIT
The fruit is made of numerous drupelets that grow together.

B SYCONIUM
The fruit axis dilates and forms a concave receptacle with the shape of a cup or bottle.

Aborted Seeds

Dry Fruits

are simple fruits whose pericarps dry as they mature. They include follicles (magnolias), legumes (peanuts, fava beans, peas), pods (radishes), and the fruits of many other species, including the majority of cereals and the fruits of trees such as maple and ash. Most dehiscent fruits (fruits that break open to expose their seeds) are dry fruits.

EXOCARP

MESOCARP

ENDOCARP

EXOCARP
The skin, or external part, of the fruit

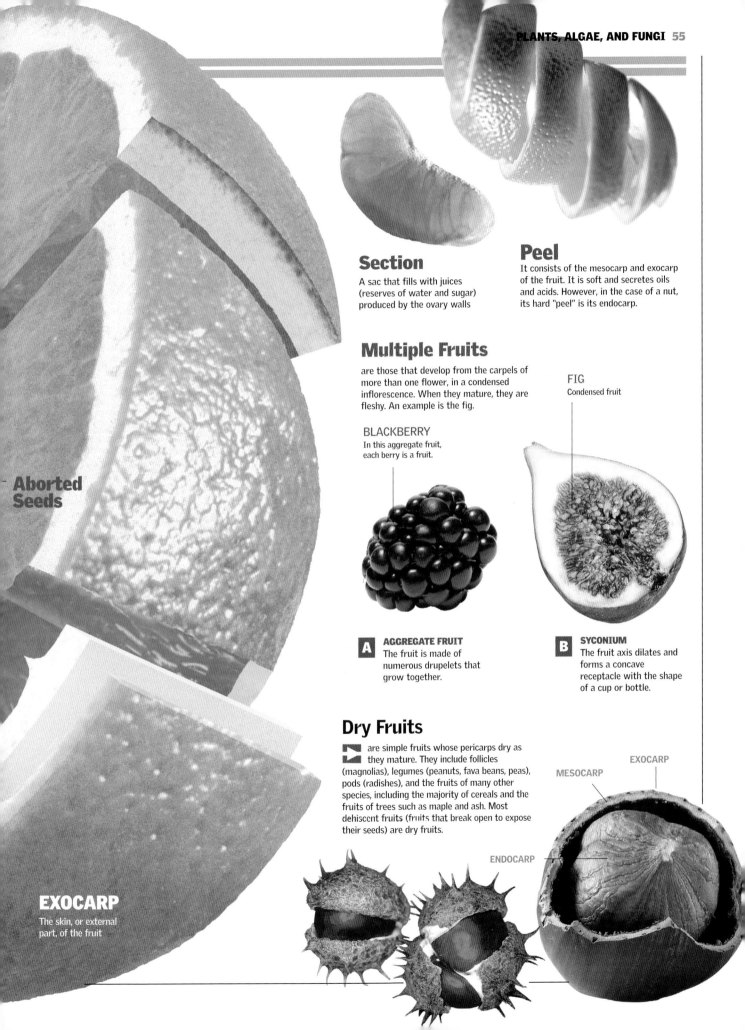

Conifers

Are effectively the most representative of the gymnosperms, a group of plants with seeds but not flowers. Through the fossil record it is known that conifers have existed for more than 390 million years. Their leaves are usually needle-shaped and perennial. They are woody plants that reproduce by means of seeds that contain tissues and an embryo that grows until it becomes an adult plant. ●

YOUNG LEAVES
are covered by a protective capsule.

FEMALE CONE
Small and light, it is likely to be pollinated as soon as it appears.

LEAVES
Grouped in sets of two, they have elongated shapes. They carry out photosynthesis.

Classification

The name "conifer" is sometimes erroneously believed to derive from pine trees' conical shape. In reality, there are other forms of coniferous plants.

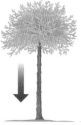

ARAUCARIA
Araucariaceae

PINE
Pinaceae

CEDAR
Taxodiaceae

CONES
The male and female cones are generally not located on the same branch.

Good Wood

The great majority of conifers are evergreens, although some, such as larches (tamarac), are deciduous. Conifers are the tallest and most long-lived trees, and they provide most of the wood used in industry. Most conifers form new shoots during the summer. They produce a resinous substance that protects them from freezing during winter. This adaptation permits vital nutrients to continue to circulate through their vascular systems, even in very cold weather.

14° F (-10° C)
OR LESS: TYPICAL AVERAGE
January temperature across the extensive coniferous forests of the Northern Hemisphere.

LEAFLET

SCALE

- Bract Scale
- Cuticle
- Gametophyte

DISPERSION

The ovuliferous scales generate a greenish gelatin containing the female gametes. The gametes are freed when the sac that contains them opens. A forest fire can promote reproduction by causing the sac to open.

Pine Cones

The female cone contains ovules that are situated among its ovuliferous scales. The cones are woody and are usually found in the upper branches of the tree. The male cones are not woody and are usually found in the lower branches. When the ovules of a female cone are pollinated, the resulting seeds need about three years to mature inside the cone. Mature ovules are popularly called pine nuts.

Bract Scales

Ovuliferous Scales

MATURE CONE

Three years after the cone appears, its seeds are ready to disseminate.

CLOSED

OPEN

Pine Nuts

Pine nuts have long been used with honey and sugar to make pastries. When summer arrives, harvested pine cones are placed in the sun, which causes them to open. The pine nuts are then shaken loose from their cones and gathered. In traditional processing the pine nuts are soaked in water to remove their outer covering, which floats to the surface. The pine nuts are then run between two closely spaced mechanical rollers to crack their inner shells. Finally, the pine-nut meat is separated from the shell by hand.

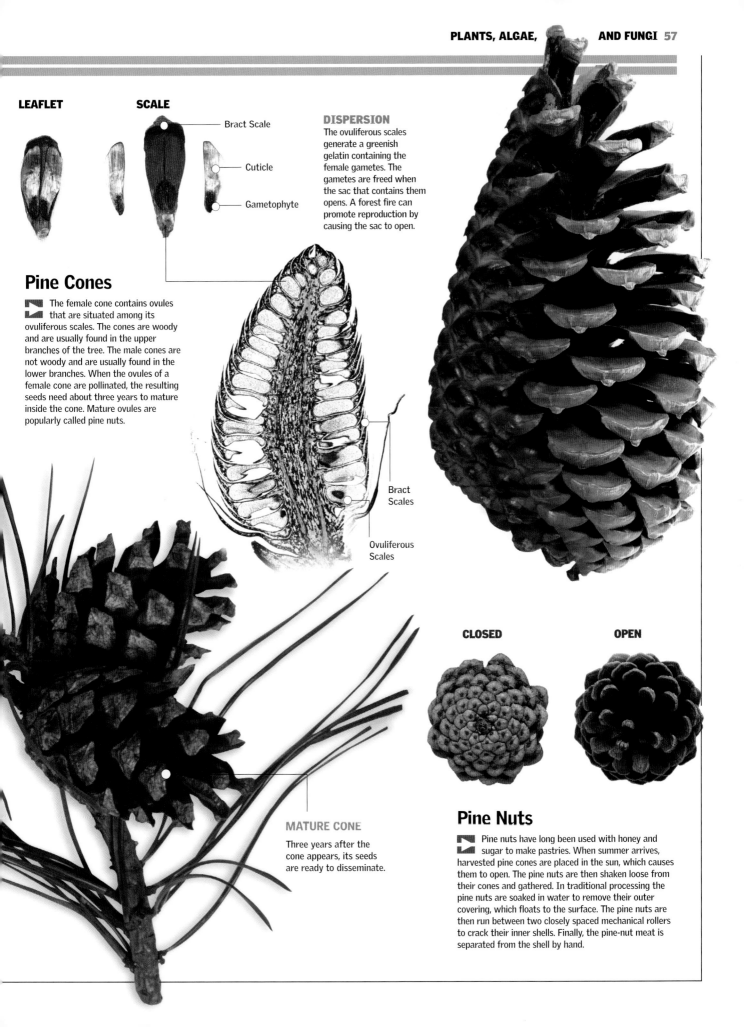

Rare and Useful Plants

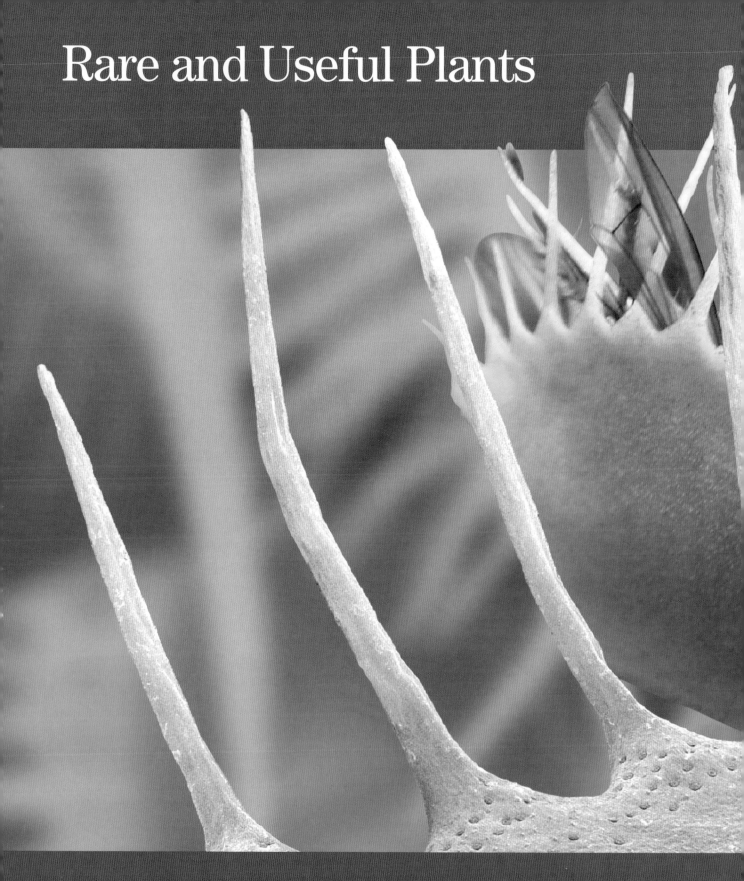

How does a carnivorous plant hunt an insect, and what type of traps does it use? Why do many plants have thorns or secrete venomous juices, while others grow on the trunks of trees or on the side of rocks? The truth is that in order to survive in harsh environments, such as places that are extremely dry or cold or places with nutrient-poor soil or

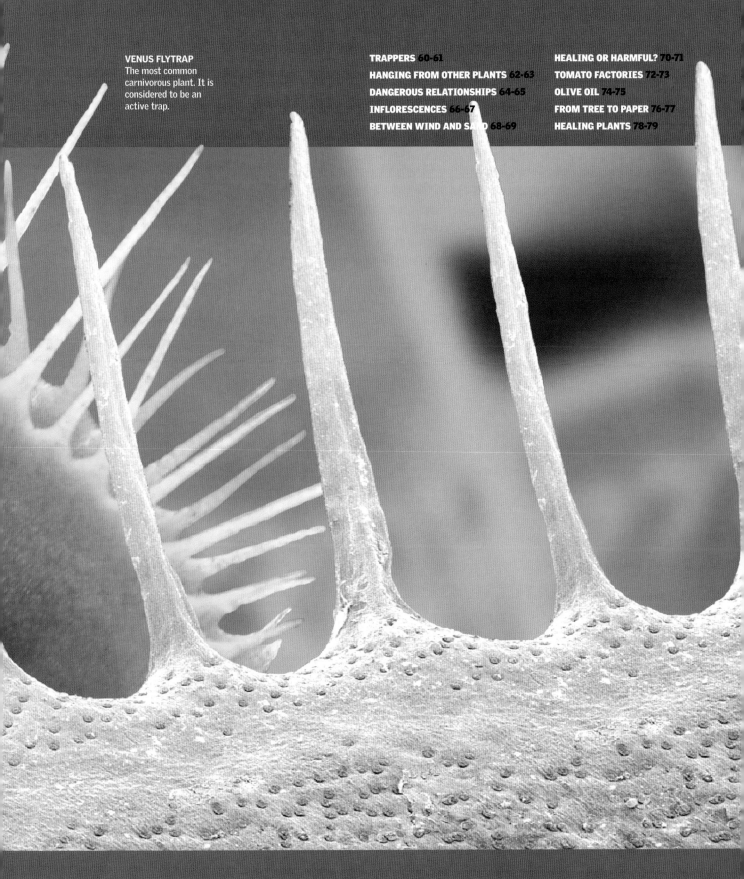

herbivorous animals, plants have had to become very strong and develop a number of strategies for survival, which we will tell you about in this chapter. You will also find detailed information about where the paper that we use daily comes from, as well as learn about the production of tomatoes and olive oil, essential elements in the human diet. ●

Trappers

These carnivorous plants are the most exotic in the entire plant kingdom. Their name is associated with their ability to capture insects and digest them. What do they get from these tiny animals? They get substances rich in nitrogen, which is usually absent from the soil where they grow. By eating insects, they are able to compensate for this nitrogen deficiency because the bodies of the arthropods they catch have amino acids and other nutrients that contain nitrogen. ●

The Terror of the Flies

The exotically named Venus flytrap is a famous carnivorous plant. It produces a nectar that attracts flies. Reaching the leaf is usually fatal for the visiting insect because it sets off a series of physiological reactions in the plant that transform it into a deadly trap. Even larger insects, such as the dragonfly, can be trapped by these carnivorous plants. Upon contact by its prey, a very specific reaction takes place. Hairs detect the presence of the insect and stimulate the closure of the leaves. However, a Venus flytrap's leaves do not react to other types of contact, such as the impact of raindrops.

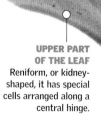

Dionaea muscipula
Scientific name of the Venus flytrap. It is native to the eastern United States.

A Varied Diet

Trappers belong to the group of autotrophic organisms—that is, they can produce organic material to use as food from simple inorganic substances. Carnivorous plants live in environments poor in nutrients. The insects that they trap permit them to make up for this deficiency.

LATERAL THORNS
are the hardened borders of the leaves, which have a thick cuticle.

DETECTOR HAIRS
are sensitive to contact with insects.

UPPER PART OF THE LEAF
Reniform, or kidney-shaped, it has special cells arranged along a central hinge.

LOWER PART OF THE LEAF
The cells have a great number of chloroplasts.

① Falling into the Trap

The fly positions itself above the trap and brushes the lateral thorns. This stimulus provokes the swollen cells of the hinge to lose water rapidly, which in turn causes the upper part of the leaf to close. If the insect is slow to react or move as the trap begins to close, it will be unable to escape.

Main Menu: Insects

There are distinct orders of dicotyledons that include carnivorous plants, such as Nepenthales, Sarraceniales, and Scrophulariales. These plants include the pitcher plant, sundews, and bladderworts.

1/5 second

THE TIME NECESSARY FOR THE UPPER PART OF THE LEAF TO CLOSE AFTER A FLY LANDS ON IT.

CARNIVOROUS PLANTS

DIONEA MUSCIPULA
Flytraps are cultivated all over the world. They are grown in slightly acidic soils, such as peat. They flourish if they have many insects to consume.

UTRICULA VULGARIS
These aquatic carnivores are of the family Lentibulariaceae. Their leaves are oval vesicles that open and close to trap microscopic animals.

DROSERA CAPENSIS
Their ribbonlike leaves are covered in sticky hairs. When the leaves receive a stimulus, they roll up and enclose the prey.

DARLINGTONIA SP.
Unlike other carnivorous pitcher plants in which the pitcher (trap) is attached to a stalk, this plant's pitcher grows directly from the soil.

SARRACENIA SP.
These plants are passive traps that use nectar to attract insects. Full of hairs, the pitchers retain the prey and keep it from escaping.

NEPENTHES MIRABILIS
The cover of its leaf-pitcher prevents water from entering. These plants tend to have very showy colors that are a fatal visual attraction to an insect.

② No Exit

The fold of the leaf stimulates the lateral thorns on its opposite sides to interlace like the fingers of two hands and create a type of cage. This process occurs in two tenths of a second, so the fly has little chance of avoiding being trapped.

③ Digestion

In less than three minutes the trap has completely closed, and the digestion of the prey's tissue begins. Special glands located in the interior part of the upper leaf secrete acids and enzymes that chemically degrade the soft parts of the insect's body. When the leaf-trap reopens after a few weeks, the wind blows away the parts of the exoskeleton that were not digested.

Hanging from Other Plants

he epiphytes are a very interesting group of plants. They grow on living or dead tree trunks, surfaces of rocks, wall nooks, and even utility poles and wires. Mosses, ferns, orchids, and bromeliads are among the best-known epiphytes. Bromeliads are native to the tropical and humid regions of the Western Hemisphere. They are of special interest because they exhibit evolutionary adaptations that favored their ability to live without contact with soil. They therefore have novel strategies for obtaining the water, minerals, carbon dioxide, and light that they need to survive.

MEDUSA'S HEAD
Tillandsia caput medusae

LEAVES
Few and leathery. They are covered in absorbent hairs.

A Different Lifestyle

Bromeliads' roots do not absorb water. Their hard leaves can capture water and nutrients from the air. Using a sticky substance, they usually attach themselves to the branches of trees, where they can have access to sunlight. These traits make it possible for the them to subsist in their natural environment.

ROOTS
They are in charge of attaching the plant to the substrate, but they do not absorb water or minerals.

BULB
The stalk is very short or nonexistent. They are herbs that form rosette-shaped bulbs with their leaves.

FLOWER
It has the form of a tube, and its color ranges from red to violet. There may be up to 14 flowers in each inflorescence.

FROM THE NEW WORLD
The common origin of the bromeliads is Mexico and the countries of Central and South America. Today bromeliads are cultivated all over the world.

Mexico
Guatemala
El Salvador
Honduras

FRUITS

Fusiform. They measure 1.5 inches (4 cm) in length and barely 0.15 inch (4 mm) in diameter. They contain feathery seeds that disperse with the wind.

SPECIAL SIGNS

These plants are recognized for their bulbs, which have the shape of a small rose, and for their triangular leaves, which are densely covered by hairs. The purple lilac color on their petals is also very characteristic.

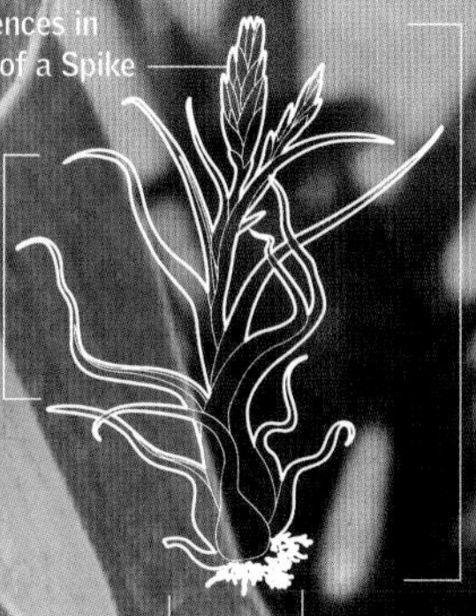

Inflorescences in the Form of a Spike

Leaves 3.5 to 5 inches (9-13 cm)

2.5 to 16 inches (6-40 cm)

1.4 to 1.6 inches (3.5-4 cm)

Special Leaves

The best-known function of these plants' leaves is to absorb water. In addition, at night they incorporate carbon dioxide and fix it into organic acids. This strategy diminishes their water loss through transpiration during the day through the opening of the stomas for gas exchange. When sunlight is available, photosynthesis takes places. The plants are able to manufacture carbohydrates without opening their stomas, because they can use the carbon dioxide that they took in during the night.

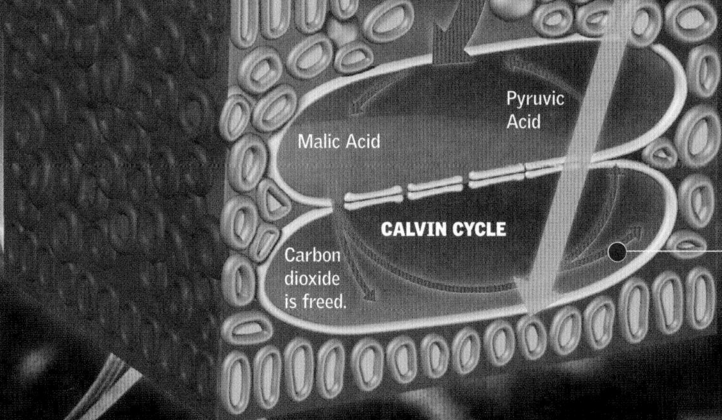

GUARD CELL opens only at night.

CARBON DIOXIDE enters during the night.

CUTICLE

DAYLIGHT

MESOPHYLL CELLS

Pyruvic Acid

Malic Acid

CALVIN CYCLE

Carbon dioxide is freed.

PRODUCTS
Phosphoglycerides that can form glucose

Dangerous Relationships

During their life cycle some plants become a true danger to other plants. There are groups of epiphytes that, in their quest to reach the soil and turn into trees, are capable of strangling and killing the tree on which they begin to grow. Additionally, some plants behave like parasites or semi-parasites. When the seeds of these plants germinate and their embryos have used up their energy reserves, they continue to grow because they obtain food from their hosts. ●

Deadly Embrace

The genus *Ficus* has some lethal plants among its members. The epiphyte species of the genus, during its young stage, can strangulate and kill the tree on which it supports itself. In this way it can reach the sunlight, which is typically scarce on the forest floor. For example, the strangler fig *(Ficus nymphaeifolia)*, which reaches 23 to 115 feet (7-35 m) in height, produces seeds that can germinate on the branches of another tree. This permits it to grow to a tree of great size that develops an extended crown of long, strong branches. Its roots descend to the ground along the trunk of the host tree and fuse together, forming a thick lattice. The distinct varieties of trees of the *Ficus* genus are characteristic of the rainforests of the intertropical zone. Many are of American origin.

SICONO

This type of infructescence is a pyriform receptacle, hollow and with an apical opening. In its internal walls small berries, commonly called seeds, are found.

IMPRISONED

The aerial roots of the straggler fig move toward the ground, perhaps as the result of geotropism. As the roots grow, they merge together and imprison the host tree.

Mistletoe

It has chlorophyll but no roots. It parasitizes the branches of a tree, disguising itself as just another branch. Mistletoe appears in places like semi-abandoned olive groves. It is native to humid zones and mountainous areas. The parasite debilitates the host and makes it more vulnerable to insect attacks. The host trees may be killed by the mistletoe or by diseases that attack the tree in its weakened state.

EUROPEAN MISTLETOE

The birds that eat mistletoe fruits disperse the seeds, which are sticky and attach to other trees.

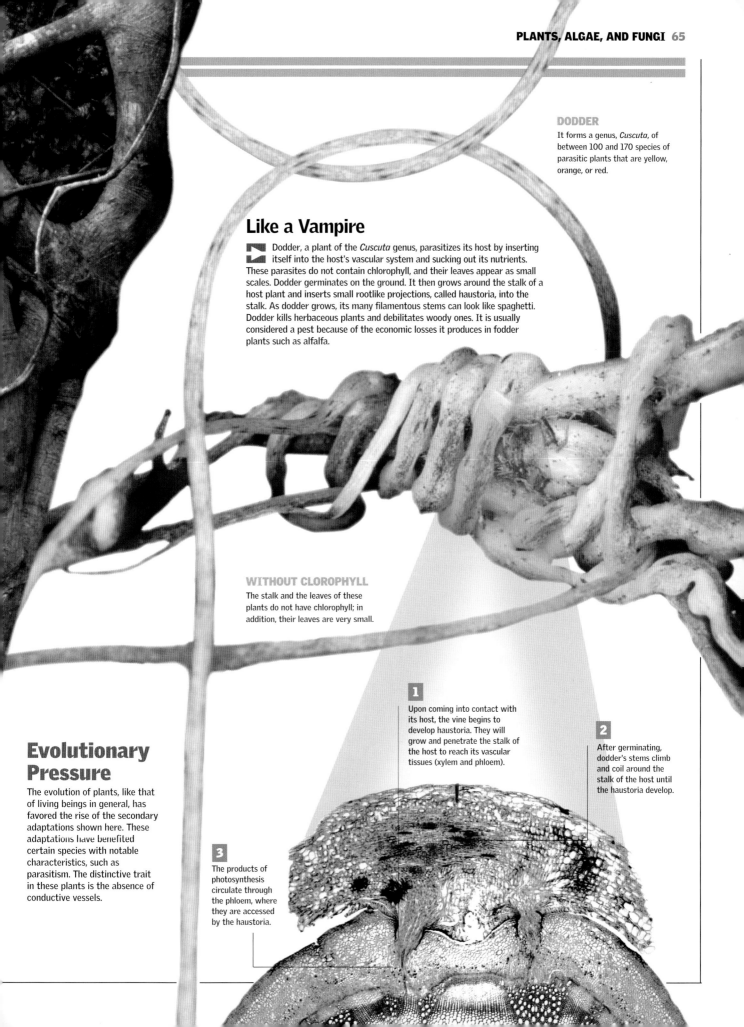

DODDER

It forms a genus, *Cuscuta*, of between 100 and 170 species of parasitic plants that are yellow, orange, or red.

Like a Vampire

Dodder, a plant of the *Cuscuta* genus, parasitizes its host by inserting itself into the host's vascular system and sucking out its nutrients. These parasites do not contain chlorophyll, and their leaves appear as small scales. Dodder germinates on the ground. It then grows around the stalk of a host plant and inserts small rootlike projections, called haustoria, into the stalk. As dodder grows, its many filamentous stems can look like spaghetti. Dodder kills herbaceous plants and debilitates woody ones. It is usually considered a pest because of the economic losses it produces in fodder plants such as alfalfa.

WITHOUT CLOROPHYLL

The stalk and the leaves of these plants do not have chlorophyll; in addition, their leaves are very small.

1
Upon coming into contact with its host, the vine begins to develop haustoria. They will grow and penetrate the stalk of the host to reach its vascular tissues (xylem and phloem).

2
After germinating, dodder's stems climb and coil around the stalk of the host until the haustoria develop.

3
The products of photosynthesis circulate through the phloem, where they are accessed by the haustoria.

Evolutionary Pressure

The evolution of plants, like that of living beings in general, has favored the rise of the secondary adaptations shown here. These adaptations have benefited certain species with notable characteristics, such as parasitism. The distinctive trait in these plants is the absence of conductive vessels.

Inflorescences

Inflorescences consist of clusters of flowers on a branch or system of branches. They can be simple or complex. They are simple when a flower forms on the main axis in the axil of each bract. They are complex when a partial inflorescence is born in the axil of the bract that also carries bracteoles or prophylls. Simple inflorescences include racemes, spikes, panicles, catkins, corymbs, and heads. Complex inflorescences include double racemes, double spikes, and double umbels. ●

Types of Inflorescences

Most inflorescences correspond to branching in which the axis grows in an indeterminate manner, and the flowers open in order from the base of the axis toward the apical meristem. There are also determinate inflorescences, in which the end of the axis bears the first flower, and flowers farthest from it open last.

Sunflower

Its inflorescence is a head made of two types of flowers: peripheral florets, which are rayed and unisexual, and disk florets, which are tubular and hermaphroditic.

RACEME
The flowers develop on short stalks, called pedicels, along an unbranched axis.

SPIKE
The flowers form directly from the stem instead of from pedicels.

HEAD
The flowers sit on a broad, shortened axis.

CORYMB
The pedicels are of varying lengths.

CATKIN
Similar to a hanging spike, its flowers are entirely male or female.

UMBEL
A group of pedicels spread from the end of the flower stalk.

COMPOUND RACEME
The flower stalks are branched.

SPADIX
It features a spike with a fleshy axis and dioecious flowers.

COMPOUND UMBEL
This form is more common than the simple umbel.

19 feet
(6m)

IS THE MAXIMUM HEIGHT OF SUNFLOWERS. THEIR AVERAGE HEIGHT IS 10 FEET (3 M).

FLAT LEAVES
Broad, oval, opposed, serrated, and rough to the touch; asperous

PERIPHERAL FLORETS

BRACTS

FLOWERS
can be fertilized
only by insects.

DISK FLORETS
Tubular and
hermaphroditic

DAISY

The daisy is a composite flower. As with the
sunflower, what appears to be a single flower is,
in fact, an inflorescence called a head. The head
contains a large number of individual flowers,
which are attached to a base called a receptacle.

Modified
Leaf

Bilobed
Stigma

Flowers with
Anthers Ready to
Release Pollen

Internal and
Immature Flower

Style

Pollen — Anther

Tubular
Corolla

Ovary

Tubular
Corolla

Ovary

LEAVES OR FLOWERS?

All flowers are modified leaves with bright colors
and attractive forms that carry out a very
specific function: attracting pollinators.

STIGMA

STYLE

OVARY

PERIPHERAL FLORETS
Rayed and unisexual

BRACTS

DOME

EPIDERMIS

MEDULLA

PEDUNCLE

POLLEN

ANTHER

NECTAR

**PERIPHERAL
FLORETS**

**DISK
FLORETS**

20,000

**THE NUMBER OF
COMPLEX PLANT
SPECIES THAT EXIST
IN THE WORLD**

Between Wind and Sand

he family Cactaceae has 300 genera and thousands of plant species that inhabit predominantly hot and dry places. Cacti are the best known of these species. They have spines that developed to minimize water loss and to provide protection against herbivores. Although cacti originated in the Western Hemisphere, they have spread to other parts of the world. Cacti produce nectar, which plays an important role in pollination by attracting insects and birds to their flowers.

Distribution

Cacti are found in deserts or very dry climates. They have also adapted to the dry and warm climates of Australia, the Mediterranean, and East Africa.

2,000 species OF PLANTS MAKE UP THE FAMILY CACTACEAE.

THEY RANGE FROM CANADA ALL THE WAY TO SOUTH AMERICA.

Cactaceae Stems

Green
In the absence of green leaves, photosynthesis takes place in the stem.

Disguised
Epiphyllum cacti do not have leaves, so the stems perform their function.

Accordion
They are curvy and expand when they take in water.

Echinopsis pentlandi

FRUIT

Generally fleshy berries. In some cases, however, the fruit is dry.

ADAPTING TO THE ENVIRONMENT

One of the main characteristics of Cactaceae is their ability to resist drought by storing water. Their roots usually extend only a short distance into the ground, which allows them to better absorb occasional rainfall. Some roots grow toward the surface in order to collect dew. Their skin is covered with wax, which makes it tough and waterproof and helps prevent water loss.

CRASSULACEAN ACID METABOLISM (CAM)

Carbon dioxide is taken in at night and stored as organic acids. The plant is therefore able to avoid water loss by closing its stomas during the day, when it carries out photosynthesis.

THICKENED STEM
Water storage

THICK EPIDERMIS
Almost poreless; avoids transpiration

VASCULAR CYLINDER
Transport tissue

SANDY SOIL
Tissue wrapping.

FLESHY ROOT
Water storage.

GOLDEN BARREL CACTUS
Echinocactus grusonii

AREOLE

Axil bud that generates a very short branching of spines

CLADODE

Photosynthetic stem, often succulent, that has the ability to store water

LEAVES

In place of simple and alternate leaves, they have thorns, which prevent water loss through transpiration and are a defense against attacks from animals.

STEM

It is succulent and stores a large quantity of water. It contains chlorophyll and is where photosynthesis takes place.

Healing or Harmful?

Poisonous plants are the type that no one wants in the garden. Although some plants have healing properties, others have substances that, when they enter the body, provoke noxious reactions that cause injury or even death. The most infamous of these plants is hemlock, which can also be used medicinally. The primary active components of poisonous plants are alkaloids. One of the most potent poisons from plants is ricin: 0.35 ounce (1 mg) is enough to kill a person.

A Matter of Quantity

Poison is a substance that produces illness or tissue lesions or that interrupts natural vital processes when it comes into contact with the human organism. Dosage is a key factor for a substance to act as a poison. The same substance that can produce death in an organism can, in smaller concentrations, act as a medicine and provide relief from certain types of suffering.

Hemlock Water Dropwort
Oenanthe crocata

A plant belonging to the Umbelliferae family that is considered toxic because of its narcotic effects. However, it can also be medically prescribed to treat disorders such as epilepsy.

Poison Hemlock
Conium maculatum

HEIGHT
It can grow to a height of 6.5 feet (2 m).

Poison Hemlock

Also known as *Conium maculatum*, this herbaceous plant belongs to the Umbelliferae family. It has a hollow, striated stem, with purple spots at its base. Though poisonous, it has been used to calm strong pains and headaches. Poison hemlock has a characteristic offensive, urinelike odor. The active component in hemlock is coniine, an alkaloid that has neurotoxic effects.

SOCRATES
This philosopher died by drinking hemlock, a sentence imposed by the Greek court.

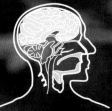

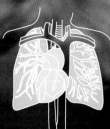

1.

BURNING

Intoxication produces a dry mouth, dilated pupils (mydriasis), and nausea.

2.

PARALYSIS

The legs weaken, the muscles become paralyzed, and respiratory failure and asphyxia take place.

3.

DEATH

The subject remains conscious until the moment of death.

Other Poisonous Plants

Several cultivated and wild plants have active ingredients that have various levels of toxicity for people and animals. The castor bean *(Ricinus communis)* contains ricin, and chewing two of its seeds can be fatal for a child. *Digitalis* contains substances that can cause a heart attack. Other common poisonous plants, such as oleanders, provoke diarrhea, nausea, and other symptoms if their flowers or fruits are eaten.

Poison Ivy

is a low vine that grows along the ground and often climbs walls, tree trunks, and bushes. It has bright green leaves that have an oily toxin, which causes light to severe allergic reactions. The symptoms can appear between one and three days after having touched the plant.

Poison Ivy
Toxicodendron radicans

HEIGHT
It can grow to a height of 10 feet (3 m).

IDENTIFICATION

In winter the plant has no leaves but greenish white berries. In the summer the berries are green; they are red in the spring and can be yellow in early autumn.

10%

OF VEGETABLE SPECIES
have alkaloids, compounds formed with nitrogen.

Belladonna (Deadly Nightshade)

has three alkaloids that are considered poisonous: hyoscine, scopolamine, and atropine. These substances affect the autonomous nervous system, which regulates breathing and cardiac rhythm. In medicine atropine in low dosages decreases the intensity of intestinal contractions.

Belladonna
Atropa belladonna

HEIGHT
It grows to a height of 5 feet (1.5 m).

WAR FLOWER

It is said that belladonna was used to poison Mark Antony's troops during the Parthian wars.

Tomato Factories

Tomato
*Solanum
lycopersicum*

The colonization of America brought about the discovery of an extraordinary variety of plants that have been used as food for a long time. An important example is the tomato, which is consumed globally. The cultivation of the tomato has reached marked levels of technological complexity that help address problems of infestation and adverse environmental conditions, as well as make it possible to grow tomatoes without using soil. ●

GREENHOUSE
Seedlings grow protected from frosts.

Traditional Cultivation

In gardens, tomato plants are grown in accordance with their annual growth cycle, using adequate soil and pest control.

Planting End of Winter

Harvesting Beginning of Summer

6 to 8 inches (15-20 cm)

5.5 pounds

(2.5 kg)

THE AVERAGE WEIGHT OF TOMATOES A PLANT CAN PRODUCE IN ONE YEAR

FERTILIZER
provides the soil with nutrients.

IRRIGATION
Every plant requires more than 0.5 gallon (2 l) of water every week as it grows.

GOOD NEIGHBORS
Raising carrot and cabbage crops in the same garden aids the development of tomatoes.

TRANSPLANT
The seedling can be transplanted when it has three or four real leaves.

STAKES
help the plants to grow and remain upright.

NETTLES
discourage insects that destroy tomatoes.

SANDY LOAM SOIL
allows for the best development of tomatoes.

LEVEL A
has nutrients that are essential to the plant.

Water Absorption Area

2 feet (0.7 m)

3 feet (1 m)

25% Lime

10% Clay

65% Sand

LEVEL B
allows for good water drainage from rain or irrigation.

LATE CROP
Transgenic tomatoes mature more slowly than tomatoes that have not been modified.

SALINE SOILS
Due to a shortage in rain, the minerals remain in Level A and increase its salinity.

LEVEL A
High concentration of salts

40% Clay

30% Sand

30% Lime

LEVEL B
The clays retain water that soaks into the soil.

MOST COMMON INFESTATIONS

Red Spider Mite
Tetranychus turkestani

Sweet Potato Whitefly
Bemisia tabaci

Green peach aphid
Myzus persicae

Transgenic Crop

Biotechnology is used to create plants that can be cultivated in soils which, under normal conditions, would not be adequate (for instance, soils with high salinity).

Planting Winter

Harvesting Summer/Autumn

3 BACTERIAL DNA
The genes are inserted into a bacterial plasmid.

4 MULTIPLICATION
Bacteria are cultivated to replicate the altered plasmids.

2 GENES
The genes that have the desired characteristic are isolated.

1 DNA
Genetic material is chosen.

5 TRANSFER
The genes are inserted into the DNA of the plant.

DRY CLIMATES
These climates are not appropriate for planting tomatoes that are not modified, but they can be used to grow modified crops.

6 NEW FRUITS
Plants are obtained that produce tomatoes with the desired characteristic.

ORIGIN OF THE TOMATO
Indigenous to Peru, it was domesticated in Mexico and Central America.

● Area of Origin
○ Main Producers

Hydroponic Cultivation

Water and nutrients are sufficient to grow tomatoes. For this reason, it is possible to grow crops in inert substrates without any soil. This technique is very useful for obtaining tomatoes in desert areas and for making them available for harvest at any time of the year.

HIGH YIELD
The cultivated fields are designed to make maximum use of the available space.

More plants per acre are desired.

64-77° F
(18-25° C)
IS THE OPTIMAL TEMPERATURE.

HYDROPONIC GREENHOUSES
allow growers to control the light, water, nutrients, and temperature of cultivation.

WATER TANK
contains water with an optimal amount of nutrients.

Drip-Control Flow Valve

The water flows under the force of gravity.

Irrigating Pipes

PUMP
Propels the water toward the irrigation tank

Troughs

COLLECTING TANK
The water is collected, and its physical and chemical properties are analyzed.

WATER
Water has long been known to be vital to plants.

SUBSTRATE
Inert materials, such as gravel or sand, work as substrates.

Olive Oil

O live oil has been a part of people's diet since antiquity, and even today it is one of the most popular oils because of its flavor and nutritious properties. Obtaining high-quality olive oil involves a chain of processes that begins at the tree and ends with the packaging of the end product. The quality begins in the fields and depends on a combination of soil, climate, oil variety, and cultivation and harvesting techniques. The remaining operations in the extraction process (transportation, storage, manufacturing, and extraction of the oil) are responsible for maintaining that quality. ●

① Cultivation

Plowed land, a moderate climate, an altitude of up to 2,300 feet (700 m) above sea level, and up to 15 inches (40 cm) of rain per year sum up the conditions needed for the development of olive plants.

NEW PLANTINGS
are propagated through staking, layering, or the taking of cuttings.

80 to 120 plants
IS THE OPTIMUM DENSITY PER ACRE (0.4 HA).

COLLECTION
Harvesting is done by hitting the tree branches, either by hand or mechanically, so that the fruits fall to the ground.

② Washing and Classification

The fruits are carefully washed with water and then classified according to their variety.

15 m

③ Milling

Machines break open the fruit and mix it to create a homogenous paste. This must be done on the day the fruit is harvested.

STONE WHEEL
Hammer systems are also used.

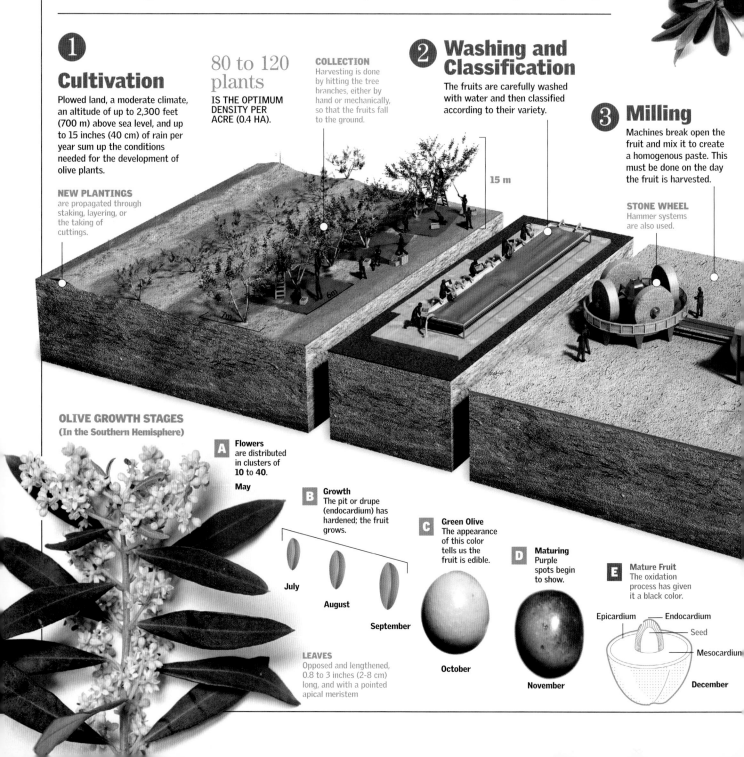

6m

7m

OLIVE GROWTH STAGES
(In the Southern Hemisphere)

A Flowers
are distributed in clusters of **10 to 40**.
May

B Growth
The pit or drupe (endocardium) has hardened; the fruit grows.

July

August

September

LEAVES
Opposed and lengthened, 0.8 to 3 inches (2-8 cm) long, and with a pointed apical meristem

C Green Olive
The appearance of this color tells us the fruit is edible.

October

D Maturing
Purple spots begin to show.

November

E Mature Fruit
The oxidation process has given it a black color.

Epicardium — Endocardium
— Seed
Mesocardium

December

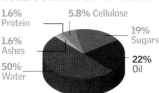

22 pounds
(10 kg)

IS THE QUANTITY OF OLIVES NEEDED TO EXTRACT **0.5 GALLON (2 L)** OF OIL.

Olive
Olea europaea

TYPES OF OIL

The classification of oil depends on the manufacturing process and on the properties of the product. The shorter the processing, the higher the quality.

Virgin Olive Oil
is obtained by pressing, without any refining. It has less than 2 percent acidity.

Refined Olive Oil
When this oil is refined, filtering soils are first added to purify it and then decanted. Its acid content is lower than that of virgin olive oil.

Olive Oil
can also be obtained by treating the residues with solvents.

COMPOSITION OF AN OLIVE

- 1.6% Protein
- 1.6% Ashes
- 50% Water
- 5.8% Cellulose
- 19% Sugars
- 22% Oil

THE QUALITY OF THE OIL

The oil that comes out of the first pressing from good quality fruits and with an acid level lower than 0.8 percent is called extra virgin. After this pressing the other levels of oil quality are obtained.

PRESS
The press has a hydraulic mechanism that compresses the disks.

DISKS
The olive paste is placed between them to be pressed.

④ Pressing

Traditionally, the paste that includes the entire olive is placed on a system of stacked discs and then compressed by a hydraulic press.

⑤ Refining

The oil obtained is separated from the other solid residues, impurities, and water. Since antiquity, this process has been carried out by decantation, which requires letting the oil sit undisturbed after it comes out of the press. Today it can also be carried out with vertical centrifugal machines.

⑥ Storage

Virgin olive oil has nonfat components that have to be preserved during storage and packaging. It must be kept in a dark place at a stable temperature.

THINGS TO AVOID

Contact with Air
Heat
Exposure to Light

FILTER
Centrifugal machines are now used.

RESIDUE
can be used to obtain other oils.

STAINLESS STEEL HOPPER
The residues are decanted at a temperature that is low, but not too low: oil crystallizes between 32° and 36° F (0°-2° C).

HOMOGENIZING
The oil from several hoppers is mixed in the final stage to obtain a uniform product.

BOTTLE
This is how the oil is sent to the market.

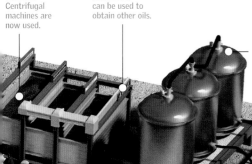

Large Residues   Residues

3 months IS THE LENGTH OF THE REFINING PERIOD.

⑦ Bottling

is carried out in a plant, although sometimes it is done manually to ensure product quality. Glass, aluminum, and plastic containers are used. It cannot be stored where it will be exposed to light, odors, or heat for extended periods.

Alternating Years

After a good crop, olive trees usually do not produce well the following year.

From Tree to Paper

The basic process of manufacturing paper has not changed for 2,000 years, although technology today allows us to manufacture paper in quantities that are immeasurably greater than those of the papyrus produced in antiquity. Paper is manufactured from a slurry that contains cellulose from tree trunks. Today the paper industry consumes 4 billion tons of wood each year. Worldwide, one of the most commonly used trees for paper manufacture is the eucalyptus because of its quick growth, its capacity to resprout trees from the stumps of young trees, its wood's quality, its consistency, and its yield. A disadvantage of eucalyptus is that it requires more water for its growth than most other trees do. ●

Wood Production by Hectare (1 ha = 2.5 ac)

300
250
50
0

Cultivation
The seedlings are obtained in greenhouses and are transplanted outdoors in furrows in the soil.

21,000 gallons
(80,000 l)
OF WATER ARE NEEDED DAILY TO IRRIGATE 1 ACRE (0.4 HA).

GROWTH RATE
After approximately 10 years the growth rate slows.

WEEDING AND FUMIGATION
eliminate weeds and other plants.

TRACTOR
Opens the furrows in the earth

0   5   10   15   Years
Initial   Maximum   Moderate

FERTILIZED
In furrows perpendicular to the incline of terrain to prevent soil erosion by the water

TRANSPLANT
The plant is placed in the center of the hole by hand.

STAKE
Helps keep the plant upright

SOIL
Claylike and siliceous, with a pH between 5 and 7

GREENHOUSE
Keeps seedlings between 69° and 80° F (21-27° C)

SEEDLINGS
are transplanted without using a hoe in order not to bend the plant.

4 billion
TONS OF WOOD IS CONSUMED EVERY YEAR.

16%
is used in paper manufacturing.

USES OF EUCALYPTUS GLOBULUS

FLOWER
In Australia the flower is most important for honey production.

LEAVES
Their resin is used in making perfumes.

Phloem   Rings   Cambium

MEDULLA
Large cells with soft-tissue walls

TRUNK
Its components provide the fiber that will be used to obtain paper.

BARK
Disposed of during the manufacturing process

Eucalyptus
Eucalyptus globulus

② Clear-Cutting

The timing of the clear-cutting will determine the financial success of the forestry venture. Replanting takes place right away.

10-13 years
IS THE OPTIMAL AGE FOR CUTTING.

CLEAR-CUTTING MACHINE
Cuts cleanly without damaging the bark

TRANSPORTATION
By trunks 8 feet (2.5 m) long

50 cubic feet (15 cu m)
IS THE AMOUNT OF WOOD PRODUCED PER HECTARE.

4 tons
IS THE AMOUNT OF WOOD NEEDED TO PRODUCE ONE TON OF CELLULOSE.

About

80,000
gallons (300,000 l)
OF WATER PER TON OF WOOD IS REQUIRED FOR THE PRODUCTION OF CARDBOARD, AND ABOUT 50,000 GALLONS OF WATER PER TON (200,000 L PER MT) OF WOOD ARE USED IN THE PRODUCTION OF PRINTING PAPER.

③ Debarking, Washing, and Splintering

The bark is separated from the trunk and eliminated from the industrial process. The debarked trunk is washed and cut into chips to facilitate handling.

DEBARKER
Machine with toothed cylinders

WASHER
Eliminates sand and impurities

CHIPPING MACHINE
The wood is cut into chips.

④ Manufacture of the Pulp

The fibers are separated and suspended in water so they can be purified and bleached.

⑤ Bleaching and Inclusion of Additives

Bleaching is done with hydrogen peroxide, oxygen, sodium hypochlorite, and other chemicals; glues, kaolin, talcum, plaster, and colorants can be added.

⑥ Forming the Paper

The mixture of pulp, suspended in water, passes into a machine with screens that hold the fibers and allow the water to drain off. Sheets of paper are the result.

⑦ Drying

Heated rotating cylinders are used to press some of the remaining water from the paper. The final moisture content depends on the type of paper being made.

DRYING ROLLERS
leave the water content of the paper between 6 and 9 percent.

⑧ Rolling and Converting

The dried paper is rolled onto reels, and the rolls are cut. The paper can later be cut into various sizes for distribution and sale.

Healing Plants

Among nature's many gifts are herbs, plants, and flowers that, since antiquity, have been used from generation to generation for therapeutic purposes. Since humans began to care for their health, these plants have been a key source of nutrition and healing. Likewise, modern medicine uses compounds derived from or obtained from herbs, roots, stems, leaves, flowers, and seeds. ●

Contributions from the New World

Various plants were found to possess an impressive number of substances that could be used for therapeutic purposes, as antibiotics, contraceptives, anesthetics, and antipyretics (fever reducers), among others. One example is quinine, used in the treatment of malaria, which was originally obtained from the bark of the quinine tree (*Chinchona* species), a tree native to South America.

ECHINACEA SP.
The medicinal plant most used by native North Americans. This plant stimulates the immune system.

SHAMANS
fulfill a central role in ancient communities as repositories of wisdom. Shamans seek to cure illnesses naturally, by means of herbs, roots, and other vegetable substances.

INDUSTRY
Echinacea is consumed around the world as a natural medicine.

Ayurvedic Medicine in India

The knowledge of life is the central principle of ayurvedic medicine. The representation of the elements that form the Universe (fire, air, water, earth, and ether) in three humors (*vata*, *pitta*, and *kapha*) indicate a person's health and temperament. The energy centers, or *chakras*, of the body are stimulated through the intake of herbs.

THE THREE TYPES OF HUMORS

Vata (wind) is associated with air and ether, *pitta* (anger) is associated with fire and water, and *kapha* (phlegm) is associated with earth and water. A holistic approach, Ayurvedic medicine provides integrated treatments that link physical care and meditation with nutrition.

VATA
(Wind)
In excess, it influences the intestines, the colon, the ears, the bones, the hips, and the skin.

DESCRIPTION
It is associated with a melancholic personality, characteristic of dreamy and erratic people.

PITTA
(Anger)
It affects the liver, gallbladder, stomach, eyes, skin, and pancreas.

DESCRIPTION
It represents a choleric personality—people who are decisive, with a tendency to embrace new ideas.

KAPHA
(Phlegm)
In excess, it can affect the throat, airways (upper and lower), and joints.

DESCRIPTION
It is associated with tranquility and serenity, typical characteristics of persons with a naturally sensitive attitude.

Chinese Medicine

The philosophy behind traditional Chinese medicine involves a qualitatively different approach from that of Western medicine. It is based on respect for the interaction between the mind, the body, energy, and the environment. Its basic principles include the five elements and the yin and yang. It is based on the concept of chi, the vital energy in equilibrium in people's bodies. Chi regulates lost equilibrium. It is under the influence of the opposing forces of yin (negative energy) and yang (positive energy). Traditional Chinese medicine includes herbal therapies, nutrition, physical exercise, meditation, acupuncture, and healing massages.

TAI CHI OR TAI JI

is the generating principle of all things, according to Chinese philosophy. It is represented with the yin and the yang, which together make up the Taoist symbol known as the "Taijitu diagram." In order to maintain good health, it is necessary to balance yin and yang.

YANG is considered male, bright, and hot.

YIN is considered female, dark, and cold.

THE THEORY OF THE FIVE ELEMENTS

Chinese tradition adds metal to the elements of the Greek model (water, fire, air, and earth). The interaction among all these elements must be kept in equilibrium, with no single element predominating over the others. Should an imbalance occur, an illness might appear.

FIRE

YIN
Motherwort (*Leonurus cardiaca*), Elecampane (*Inula helenium*), English lavender (*Lavandula angustifolia*)
YANG
Hawthorn (*Crataegus oxyacantha*), sour orange (*Citrus aurantium*), meadowsweet (*Filipendula ulmaria*)

Bitter Herbs
Their action is focused on the heart and the small intestine. They lower fevers and sensations of heat, and they redirect vital energy, or chi.

Sweet Herbs
are tonic and nutritious. They harmonize with other herbs, relieve pain, and stop the progression of severe illnesses.

YIN
Garden angelica (*Angelica archangelica*), Italian cyprus (*Cupressus sempervirens*), common hop (*Humulus lupulus*), rosemary (*Rosmarinus officinalis*)
YANG
Greater plantain (*Plantago major*), dandelion (*Taraxacum officinale*), marjoram (*Origanum majorana*)

WOOD

YIN
Chamomile (*Matricaria chamomilla*), cinnamon (*Cinnamomum zeylanicum*), yellow gentian (*Gentiana lutea*), Minor centaury (*Centaurium umbellatum*)
YANG
Lemon (*Citrus limonum*), common juniper (*Juniperus communis*), lemon balm (*Melissa officinalis*), cranberry (*Vaccinium myrtillus*), olive (*Olea europaea*)

EARTH

Salty Herbs
are refreshing; they soften hard spots, lubricate the intestines, and promote their emptying. They reduce constipation, kidney stones, gout, etc.

Sour Herbs
basically act on the liver and the gallbladder. They activate bilious secretions.

YIN
Heather (*Calluna vulgaris*), blessed milk thistle (*Silybum marianum*), ginseng (*Panax ginseng*)

Spicy Herbs
induce sweating, blood circulation, and chi, or vital energy. They are generally used for superficial disorders.

YIN
Ginger (*Zingiber officinale*), peppermint (*Mentha piperita*), thyme (*Thymus vulgaris*)

Ginger

YANG
Shepherd's purse (*Capsella bursa-pastoris*), red sandwort (*Arenaria rubra*), rough bindweed (*Smilax aspera*)

YANG
Corn poppy (*Papaver rhoeas*), Tasmanian bluegum (*Eucalyptus globulus*), common borage (*Borago officinalis*)

WATER

METAL

Fungi

For nearly a billion years the ability of fungi to break down substances has been important to life on Earth. These life-forms break down carbon compounds and return carbon and other elements to the environment to be used by other organisms. They interact with roots, enabling them to better absorb water and mineral

AMANITA MUSCARIA
The quintessential toadstool has unpleasant psychoactive effects. Depending on the dose, they range from dizziness, muscle cramps, and vomiting to amnesia.

nutrients. For many years fungi were classified within the plant kingdom. However, unlike plants, they cannot produce their own food. Many are parasites. Some fungi are pathogens— they can cause sickness in humans, animals, or plants. ●

Another World

For many years fungi were classified within the plant kingdom. However, unlike plants, they are heterotrophic—unable to produce their own food. Some fungi live independently, whereas others are parasitic. Like animals, they use glycogen for storing reserves of energy, and their cell walls are made of chitin, the substance from which insects' outer shells are made. ●

Fungi: A Peculiar Kingdom

Fungi can develop in all sorts of environments, especially damp and poorly lit places, up to elevations of 13,000 feet (4,000 m). They are divided into four large phyla, in addition to a group of fungi called "imperfect" because they generally do not reproduce sexually. At present, 15,000 species of fungi fall into this category. DNA analysis has recently reclassified them as Deuteromycetes.

Chytridiomycota

are the only fungi that, at some point in their lives, have mobile cells—male and female gametes, which they release into water in order to reproduce. They live in water or on land, feeding on dead material or living as parasites on other living organisms. Their cell walls are made of chitin.

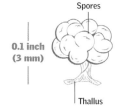

Spores

0.1 inch (3 mm)

Thallus

VARIETY
There are great anatomical differences among the Chytridiomycetes. In the same reproductive phase they can produce haploid and diploid spores.

39° to 140° F

(4°-60° C)
THE TEMPERATURE RANGE IN WHICH MOST FUNGI CAN LIVE IN HUMID CLIMATES

Spores

Slime Mold
Physarum polycephalum

Deuteromycota

are also called "imperfect fungi" because they are not known to have a form of sexual reproduction. Many live as parasites on plants, animals, or humans, causing ringworm or mycosis on the skin. Others–such as *Penicillium*, which produces penicillin, and *Cyclospora*–have great medicinal and commercial value.

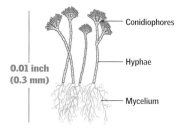

Conidiophores

Hyphae

0.01 inch (0.3 mm)

Mycelium

OF UNKNOWN SEX
In Deuteromycetes, conidia are tiny spores that function asexually. They are contained in structures called conidiophores.

Basidiomycota

This phylum, which includes mushrooms, is the most familiar of the fungi. The mushroom's reproductive organ is its cap. Its branches grow underground or into some other organic substrate.

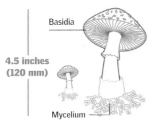

Basidia

CAPPED MUSHROOMS
With its recognizable shape, the mushroom's cap protects the basidia, which produce spores.

4.5 inches (120 mm)

Mycelium

Chanterelle Mushroom
Cantharellus cibarius

Black Bread Mold
Rhizopus nigricans

80,857

DIFFERENT SPECIES
HAVE BEEN IDENTIFIED IN THE FUNGI KINGDOM. THERE ARE BELIEVED TO BE APPROXIMATELY 1,500,000 SPECIES.

Zygomycota

is a phylum of land-growing fungi that reproduce sexually with zygosporangia, diploid cells that do not break their cell walls until conditions are right for germinating. They also reproduce asexually. Most zygomycetes live in the soil and feed on plants or dead animal matter. Some live as parasites on plants, insects, or small land animals.

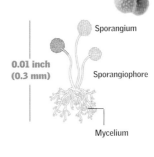

Sporangium

0.01 inch (0.3 mm)

Sporangiophore

Mycelium

MANY LITTLE POUCHES
Its spores are formed when two gametes of opposite sexes fuse. It can also reproduce asexually, when the sporangium breaks and releases spores.

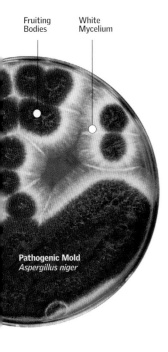

Fruiting Bodies

White Mycelium

Pathogenic Mold
Aspergillus niger

Ascus with Ascospores

Ascomycota

is the phylum with the most species in the Fungi kingdom. It includes yeasts and powdery mildews, many common black and yellow-green molds, morels, and truffles. Its hyphae are partitioned into sections. Their asexual spores (conidia) are very small and are formed at the ends of special hyphae.

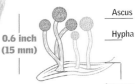

EXPLOSIVE
At maturity the asci burst. The explosion releases their sexual spores (ascospores) into the air.

Ascus

Hypha

0.6 inch (15 mm)

Ascocarp

Ergot
Claviceps purpurea

The Diet of Fungi

Fungi do not ingest their food like animals. On the contrary, they absorb it after breaking it down into small molecules. Most of them feed on dead organic material. Other fungi are parasites, which feed on living hosts, or predators, which live off the prey they trap. Many others establish relationships of mutual benefit with algae, bacteria, or plants and receive organic compounds from them. ●

Chemical Transformation

The organic or inorganic substances that fungi feed on are absorbed directly from the environment. Fungi first secrete digestive enzymes onto the food source. This causes a chemical transformation that results in simpler, more easily assimilated compounds. Basidiomycetes are classified according to their diet. For example, they colonize different parts of a tree depending on the nutrients they require.

PARASITES
Fungi such as *Ceratocystis ulmi* and *Agrocybe aegerita* (shaded areas on the leaf) live at the expense of other plants, which they can even kill. Others live parasitically off animals.

SAPROBES
There is no organic material that cannot be broken down by this type of fungus. They actually live on the dead parts of other plants, so they cause no harm to the host.

SYMBIOTIC
While feeding off the plant, they help it to obtain water and mineral salts more easily from the soil. Each species has its own characteristics.

CAP
Besides being easy to spot, the cap is the fertile part of basidiomycetes; it contains spores.

Fungi of the genus *Amanita*, including the poisonous *A. muscaria* shown here, have the well-known mushroom shape with a mushroom cap.

MYCELIUM
When a mushroom spore finds the right medium, it begins to generate a network of hyphae, branching filaments that extend into the surrounding medium. This mass of hyphae is called a mycelium. A mushroom forms when threads of the mycelium are compacted and grow upward to create a fruiting body.

Spore-producing structures

Hyphae

FRUITING BODY
The basidiocarp, or mushroom cap, generates new spores.

VEGETATIVE MYCELIUM
It is made of branches of threadlike hyphae that grow underground.

CUTICLE

The skin, or membrane, that covers the cap, or pileus, is called the cuticle. It can have a variety of colors and textures, such as velvety, hairy, scaly, threadlike, fibrous, fuzzy, smooth, dry, or slimy.

GILLS

are the structures that produce spores. Their shape varies according to the species.

BASIDIA

are fine structures that contain groups of four cells, which are able to reproduce.

Basidium

Basidiospore

HYMENIUM

It is located on the underside of the cap. It contains very fine tissues that produce spores. Its structure can consist of tubes, wrinkles, hairlike projections, or even needles.

Detail of a Gill

LIFE CYCLE OF A FUNGUS

Fungi produce spores during sexual or asexual reproduction. Spores serve to transport the fungus to new places, and some help the fungus to survive adverse conditions.

Development of the fruit-bearing body

Spore formation by fertilization

Hyphae formation

Release of spores

RING

Also known as the veil, it protects part of the hymenium in young fungi.

Growth

At birth the fruiting body of the species *Amanita muscaria* looks like a white egg. It grows and opens slowly as the mushroom's body unfolds. As it grows the cap first appears completely closed. During the next several days it opens like an umbrella and acquires its color.

STEM

Cylindrical in shape, it holds up the cap and reveals important information for identifying the species.

Did You Know?

Fungi can break down an impressive variety of substances. For example, a number of species can digest petroleum, and others can digest plastic. Fungi also provided the first known antibiotic, penicillin. They are now a basic source of many useful medical compounds. Scientists are studying the possibility of using petroleum-digesting fungi to clean up oil spills and other chemical disasters.

HALLUCINOGENIC MUSHROOM
Psilocybin aztecorum

VOLVA

The volva is made of the remains of the early rings that have fallen off. It differs from species to species.

Strobilurus esculentus

lives on the cones of various pine trees.

Poison in the Kingdom

A poisonous fungus is one that, when ingested, causes toxic effects. In terms of its effects on the eater, the toxicity can vary according to the species and to the amount ingested. At times poisoning is not caused by eating fungi but by eating foods, such as cereal products, that have been contaminated by a fungus. Rye, and to a lesser extent oats, barley, and wheat, can host toxic fungi that produce dangerous mycotoxins. These mycotoxins can cause hallucinations, convulsions, and very severe damage in the tissues of human organs. ●

ERGOTISM (ST. ANTHONY'S FIRE)

Attack on Rye

Ergot (*Claviceps purpurea*) is a parasite of rye and produces alkaloid mycotoxins—ergocristine, ergometrine, ergotamine, and ergocryptine. When barley with ergot is processed for use in food, the mycotoxins can be absorbed when eaten. All these toxic substances can act directly on nerve receptors and cause the constriction of blood vessels.

2.
Fruit

The perithecium is a type of fruiting, or reproductive, body in ascomycetes. It is a type of closed ascocarp with a pore at the top. The asci are inside the perithecium.

3.
Spores

The asci are sac-shaped cells that contain spores called ascospores. In general, they grow in groups of eight and are light enough to be scattered into the air.

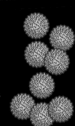

1.
Release

Within the enclosing structures a stroma, or compact somatic body, is formed. Inside it reproductive growths develop, which contain a large number of perithecia.

Ergotism

Ergotism, or St. Anthony's Fire, is a condition caused by eating products such as rye bread that have been contaminated with alkaloids produced by *Claviceps purpurea* fungi, or ergot. The alkaloids typically affect the nervous system and reduce blood circulation in the extremities, which produces the burning sensation in the limbs that is one of the condition's notable symptoms.

INGESTION
The main means of intake of the mycotoxins is through products manufactured with flour.

NERVOUS SYSTEM
Lethargy, drowsiness, and more severe conditions, such as convulsions, hallucinations, and blindness, are symptoms caused by the effects of ergot on the nervous system.

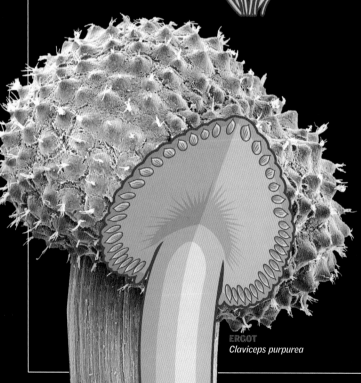

ERGOT
Claviceps purpurea

EXTREMITIES
Ergotamine alkaloids cause the constriction of blood vessels, leading to gangrene.

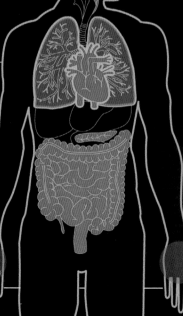

Poisonous Mushrooms

Eating the fruiting bodies of some species can be very dangerous if it is not clearly known which are edible and which are poisonous. There is no sure method for determining the difference. However, it is known for certain that some species–such as certain species of the genera *Amanita, Macrolepiota*, and *Boletus*–are poisonous.

DESTROYING ANGEL
Amanita virosa

4.

Parasites

Ascospores of sexual origin or asexual conidia develop as parasites in the ovary of the rye flower. They cause the death of its tissues and form sclerotia. In some languages ergot's name is related to the word for "horn" because of sclerotia's hornlike shape.

Pretty But Deadly

This mushroom is toxic to the liver. It grows from spring to fall, often in sandy, acidic soil in woodlands and mountainous regions. Its cap is white and 2 to 5 inches (5-12 cm) in diameter. Its stem and gills are also white, and the gills may appear detached from the stem. The base of the stem has a cuplike volva, but it may be buried or otherwise not visible.

Insecticide

The fly agaric's name is thought to come from its natural fly-killing properties. Its cap is typically red and 6 to 8 inches (15-20 cm) in diameter. It may be covered with white or yellow warts, but they are absent in some varieties. The stem is thicker at the base, which looks cottony. It also has a large white ring that looks like a skirt. It grows in summer and fall in coniferous and deciduous forests. If eaten, it causes gastrointestinal and psychotropic symptoms.

RYE BREAD

WHISKEY

FLOUR

FLY AGARIC
Amanita muscaria

Derived from Rye

In Europe during the Middle Ages wheat bread was a costly food, not part of the common diet. Most people ate bread and drank beer prepared from rye. This made them susceptible to ingesting mycotoxins from *Claviceps purpurea*. Thus, the largest number of cases of ergotism occurred during this time. Today preventative controls in the production of bread and related products from rye and other cereals have greatly reduced instances of ergotism.

Pathogens

F ungi that are able to cause illnesses in people, animals, or plants are called pathogens. The nocive, or toxic, substances that these organisms produce have negative effects on people and cause significant damage to agriculture. One reason these pathogens are so dangerous is their high tolerance to great variations in temperature, humidity, and pH. *Aspergillus* is a genus of fungi whose members create substances that can be highly toxic. ●

CONIDIA CHAIN
Conidia are asexual spores that form at the ends of the hyphae. In this case they group together in chains.

CONIDIA
are so small that they spread through the air without any difficulty.

900

THE NUMBER OF *ASPERGILLUS* SPECIES. THEY HAVE BEEN CLASSIFIED INTO 18 GROUPS. MOST OF THESE SPECIES ARE ASSOCIATED WITH HUMAN ILLNESSES, SUCH AS ASPERGILLOSIS.

PHIALIDES
are cells from which conidia are formed.

CONIDIOPHORE
The part of the mycellium of the fruiting, or reproductive, body in which asexual spores, or conidia, are formed

ALLERGENICS *Aspergillus flavus*

This species is associated with allergic reactions in people with a genetic predisposition to this allergy. They also cause the contamination of seeds, such as peanuts. They produce secondary metabolites, called micotoxins, that are very toxic.

SAPROBIA *Aspergillus* sp.

In addition to the pathogen species, there are some species of *Aspergillus* that decompose the organic matter of dead insects, thus incorporating nutrients into the soil.

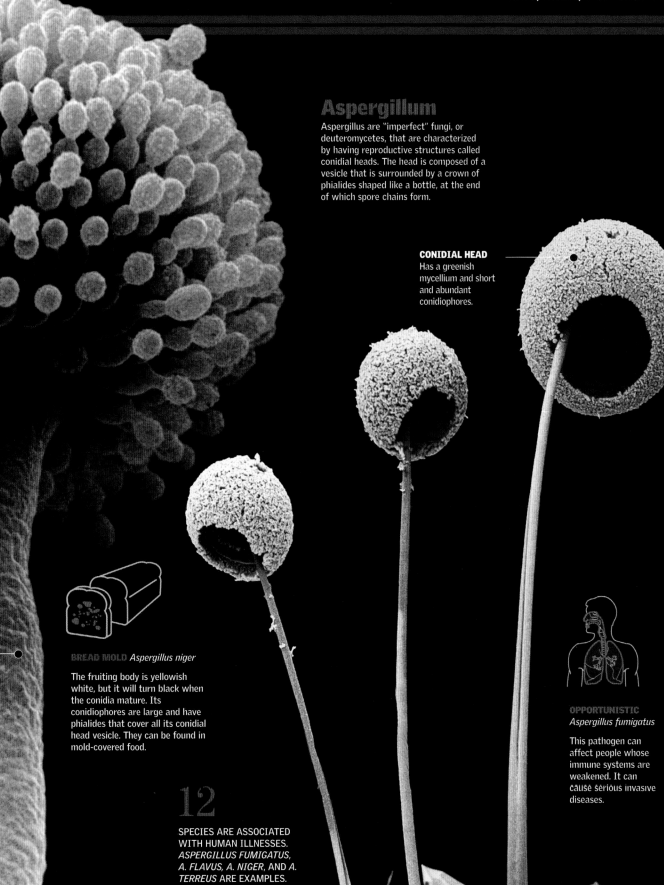

Aspergillum

Aspergillus are "imperfect" fungi, or deuteromycetes, that are characterized by having reproductive structures called conidial heads. The head is composed of a vesicle that is surrounded by a crown of phialides shaped like a bottle, at the end of which spore chains form.

CONIDIAL HEAD
Has a greenish mycellium and short and abundant conidiophores.

BREAD MOLD *Aspergillus niger*

The fruiting body is yellowish white, but it will turn black when the conidia mature. Its conidiophores are large and have phialides that cover all its conidial head vesicle. They can be found in mold-covered food.

12

SPECIES ARE ASSOCIATED WITH HUMAN ILLNESSES. *ASPERGILLUS FUMIGATUS, A. FLAVUS, A. NIGER*, AND *A. TERREUS* ARE EXAMPLES.

OPPORTUNISTIC
Aspergillus fumigatus

This pathogen can affect people whose immune systems are weakened. It can cause serious invasive diseases.

Destroying to Build

Yeast
*Saccharomyces
cerevisiae*

Yeasts, like other fungi, decompose organic material. This capacity can be beneficial, and, in fact, human beings have developed yeast products for home and industrial use, such as bread, baked goods, and alcoholic beverages, that attest to its usefulness. Beer manufacturing can be understood by analyzing how yeasts feed and reproduce and learning what they require in order to be productive. ●

Precious Gems

Yeast from the genus *Sacchromyces cerevisiae* can reproduce both asexually and sexually. If the concentration of oxygen is adequate, the yeasts will reproduce sexually, but if oxygen levels are drastically reduced, then gemation will take place instead. Gemation is a type of asexual proliferation that produces child cells that split off from the mother cell. Starting with barley grain, this process produces water, ethyl alcohol, and a large quantity of CO_2, the gas that forms the bubbles typically found in beer.

Fermentation

Under anaerobic conditions yeasts can obtain energy and produce alcohol. By means of the alcoholic fermentation process they obtain energy from pyruvic acid, a product of the breakdown of glucose by glucolysis. In this process CO_2 is also produced and accumulated, as is ethyl alcohol. The carbon dioxide will be present in the final product: the beer.

WINE YEAST
Yeast is also used to produce wine. In wine production, however, the CO_2 that is produced is eliminated.

WINE YEAST
Yeast
*Saccharomyces
ellipsoideus*

2 SPORES
A sac called an ascus is formed that contains ascospores of yeast.

1 MEIOSIS
A diploid cell forms four haploid cells.

3 RELEASE OF THE ASCOSPORES
The opening of the ascus releases the spores, which then reproduce by mitosis.

Cycle

GROW AND MULTIPLY
As long as they have adequate nutrients, yeasts will continuously repeat their reproductive life cycle.

6 MULTIPLICATION
A large number of cells are produced in this stage.

4 UNION OF THE ASCOSPORES
The haploid cells fuse and form a new diploid cell.

5 GEMATION
Under the right conditions the diploid cells begin to reproduce asexually.

Homemade Bread

Many products are made with yeasts, and one of the most important is bread. In the case of bread, yeasts feed off the carbohydrates present in flour. Bread products, unlike alcoholic beverages, need to have oxygen available for the yeast to grow. The fungi release carbon dioxide as they quickly consume the nutrients. The bubbles of carbon dioxide make the dough expand, causing the bread to rise.

NUCLEUS
It coordinates all the cell's activities. Its duplication is vital in making each child cell the same as its progenitor cell.

MITOCHONDRIA
These subcellular structures become very active when the cell is in an environment rich in oxygen.

CELL MEMBRANE
The cell membrane controls what enters or exits the cell. It acts as a selective filter.

GEMATION
Buds, or gems, which will become independent in a new cell, are formed in different parts of a yeast.

12%

THE MAXIMUM PERCENTAGE OF ALCOHOL THAT YEAST WILL TOLERATE

ENZYME PRODUCTION
Internal membrane systems produce the enzymes that regulate the production of alcohol and carbon dioxide in the cells.

VACUOLE
This organelle contains water and minerals that are used in the cell's metabolism. The concentration of these nutrients helps regulate the activity of the cell.

Glossary

Adventitious Root

Root that appears in unusual places, such as on the stem

Algae

Organisms of the Protist kingdom, at one time considered plants, but without roots, stems, or leaves. They live in water or in humid areas. They can be pluricellular or unicellular.

Allele

Gene variant that encodes a trait. One diploid cell contains one allele from each parent for each characteristic.

Anaerobic

Reaction, or series of reactions, that does not require oxygen

Analogy

Similarity produced in similar environments through the adaptation of species that do not have a common ancestor

Angiosperms

From the Greek *angion* (recipient) and *sperm* (seed). Plants with flowers whose seeds are contained in structures that develop into fruits.

Anther

Structure of the stamen composed of two locules and four pollen sacs

Asexual Reproduction

Process through which a single progenitor generates descendants identical to itself

ATP

Adenosine triphosphate. Molecule produced by the mitochondria, which functions as the main source of energy for cells.

Berry

Simple fleshy fruit formed by one or more carpels

Biome

Ecosystem that occupies a large area and is characterized by specific types of vegetation

Bryophytes

Group of small flowerless plants that comprise the hepaticae, anthocerotae, and mosses

Bulb

Modified structure of the stem in which starch accumulates in thickened leaves

Cambium

Interior part of the root and the stem of a plant that forms xylem on one side and phloem on the other. It makes stems grow thicker.

Carpel

Female part that bears the ovules of a flower. The grouping of carpels forms the gynoecium.

Cell

Smallest vital unit of an organism. Plant cells have a wall that is more or less rigid.

Cellular Membrane

Flexible cover of all living cells. It contains cytoplasm and regulates the exchange of water and gases with the exterior.

Cellular Respiration

Aerobic processes that extract energy from food, including glycolysis, oxidative phosphorylation, and the Krebs cycle. Eukaryote cells carry out these processes in the cytoplasm and the mitochondria.

Cellulose

Fibrous carbohydrate that a plant produces as part of its structural material. Main component of the cell wall.

Chitin

Polysaccharide that contains nitrogen. It is present in the cell walls of mushrooms.

Chlorophyll

Pigment contained in the chloroplasts of plant cells. It captures the energy of light during photosynthesis.

Chloroplast

Microscopic sac, located on the inside of green-plant cells, where the chemical processes of photosynthesis take place

Cilium

Short external appendage that propels a cell and is composed of microtubules

Class

Taxonomic group superior to order and inferior to phylum. For example, the Charophyceae class includes green algae related to higher plants.

Cotyledon

First leaf of flowering plants, found on the inside of the seed. Some store food and remain buried while the plant germinates.

Cytoplasm

Compartment of the cells of eukaryotes, marked by the cellular membrane and the membranes of the organelles of the cell

Deciduous

Describes a plant that loses all its leaves in specific seasons of the year

Dicotyledon

Flowering plant whose seed has two cotyledons

Diploid

Cell with two complete sets of chromosomes

DNA

Deoxyribonucleic acid. Double helix molecule with codified genetic information.

Drupe

Simple fleshy fruit that develops from hypogynous flowers—flowers in which the ovary lies above the point where the other flower parts are attached. It has one seed in its interior. Examples include the olive, peach, and almond.

Ecosystem

Grouping of the organisms of a community and the nonbiological components associated with their environment

Embryo

Product of an egg cell fertilized by a sperm cell; it can develop until it constitutes an adult organism.

Endodermis

Layer of specialized cells, composed of thicker cells; in young roots it is found between the bark and the vascular tissues.

Endoplasmic Reticulum

Network of membranes connected through the cytoplasm that serves as a site of synthesis and assembly for the cell to form its proteins

Enzyme

Protein that helps to regulate the chemical processes in a cell

Epidermis

The most external cellular layers of stems and leaves

Epiphyte

Plant that grows and supports itself on the surface of another plant but does not take water or nutrients from it

Family

Taxonomic category, inferior to order, that groups the genera

Fertilization

Fusion of the special reproductive cells (contained in the pollen and in the ovules) in order to give rise to a new plant

Filament

Structure, in the form of a thread, that forms the support of a flower's stamen

Fruit

Ovary or group of ovaries of a flower, transformed and mature. It contains the seeds.

Gametangium

Unicellular or multicellular structure from which the gametes, or reproductive sexual cells, originate

Gene

Unit of information of a chromosome. Sequence of nucleotides in the DNA molecule that carries out a specific function.

Genetic Drift

Phenomenon produced in small populations that demonstrates that the frequency of alleles can vary by chance or throughout generations

Germination

Process in which a plant begins to grow from a seed or a spore

Gymnosperm

Plants with seeds that are not sealed in an ovary. Examples are conifers (pine, fir, larch, cypress).

Gynoecium

Grouping of carpels of a flower that make up the female sexual organ of angiosperms

Haploid

From the Greek *haplous*, singular: cell with one set of chromosomes, unlike diploids. It is characteristic of the gametes, the gametophytes, and some mushrooms.

Haustoria

Vessels with which some parasitic plants penetrate other species in order to feed themselves from substances photosynthesized by the host

Host

Plant from which another organism (parasite) obtains food or shelter

Hyphae

Interwoven filaments that form the mycelium of fungi

Inflorescence

Groupings of flowers in a specific form on a peduncle

Kingdom

Taxonomic group superior to a phylum and inferior to a domain, such as the kingdom Plantae

Legume

Simple fruit of some species that come from one carpel divided in two. Examples are garbanzos and peas.

Lichen

The symbiotic union of a fungus and an alga; the food is synthesized by the algae and used by the fungus, which offers the alga a moist and protected habitat in which to live.

Lignin

A substance related to cellulose that helps form the woody parts of plants

Ligula

Petal developed on the border of the head of certain composite flowers. Its color may be blue or yellow, or more commonly, white, as in the case of daisies.

Macronutrient

Essential chemical element that a plant needs in relatively large quantities and that is involved in its vital processes. Examples are nitrogen and phosphorus.

Medulla

Basic tissue formed inside the vascular tissue

Meiosis

Type of cellular division in which two successive divisions of the diploid nucleus of a cell give rise to four haploid nuclei. As a result, gametes or spores are produced.

Meristem

Region of tissue consisting of cells that produce other cells through cellular division

Mitochondria

Organelle delimited by a double membrane. In it, the final stage of aerobic respiration is carried out, in which ATP is obtained from the decomposition of sugars.

Mitosis

Nuclear division that forms two descendant nuclei identical to the progenitor

Molecular Clock

Marker used to calculate the evolutionary distance between two species. It is evaluated by comparing the gradual accumulation of differences in amino acids among the proteins of each species.

Monocotyledons

Flowering plants with only one cotyledon. Examples are the onion, orchid, and palm.

Mycelium

Interwoven mass of hyphae of a fungus

Nectar

Sweet liquid, produced by flowers and some leaves, that attracts insects and birds, which serve as pollinating agents

Node

Axillary bud, the part of the stem of a plant where one or more leaves appear

Nucellus

Structure located inside plants with seeds, where the embryonic sac is developed

Nucleic Acid

A molecule that carries genetic information about the cell

Nucleus

The part of the cell that contains the DNA, which carries the genetic material

Osmosis

The movement of a liquid through a selectively permeable membrane

Ovary

The part of a flower consisting of one or more carpels and containing the ovules. Fertilized, it will form all or part of the fruit.

Ovule

The part of the ovary in flowering plants that contains the female sexual cells. After fertilization it transforms into seed.

Parasite

An organism that lives at the expense of another, from which it obtains its nutrients

Petal

Modified leaves that form the corolla

Phloem

Vessels that conduct the sap throughout the entire plant

Photorespiration

Process through which some plants close their stomas in order to avoid dehydration

Photosynthesis

Process through which the energy of light is used to produce carbohydrates from carbon dioxide and water

Phytoplankton

Group of free-living microscopic aquatic organisms with the capacity to carry out photosynthesis

Pollen

Fine powder of plants with seeds whose grains contain the male sexual cells

Pollination

Passage of pollen from the male organ of a flower to the female organ of the same flower or another

Polymer

Macromolecule formed from repeated structural units called monomers

Polypeptide

Polymer of amino acids; examples are proteins.

Protein

Macromolecule composed of one or more chains of amino acids. They define the physical characteristics of an organism and regulate its chemical reactions when they act as enzymes.

Protoplast

Plant cell without a cell wall

Rhizoids

Cellular formation or filament in the form of a thin and branching tube that attaches mosses to the soil

Rhizome

Horizontal subterranean stem

Ribosome

Organelle located in the cytoplasm that directs the formation of proteins on the basis of information given by the nucleic acids

Root

Organ that fixes a plant to the soil and absorbs water and minerals from it

Sap

Watery liquid that contains the products of photosynthesis and is transported by the phloem

Seed

Structure consisting of the embryo of a plant, a reserve of food called the endosperm, and a protective cover called the testa

Seedling

First sprouting of the embryo of a seed, formed by a short stem and a pair of young leaves

Sepal

Modified leaf that forms the outer covering of a flower that protects the bud before it opens

Sexual Reproduction

Reproduction based on the fertilization of a female cell by a male cell; it produces descendants different from both progenitors.

Sori

Set of sporangia found on the underside of fern leaves

Spore

Reproductive structure formed by one cell, capable of originating a new organism without fusing with another cell

Sporangia

Structure in which spores are formed

Stamen

Element of the male reproductive apparatus of a flower that carries pollen. It is formed by a filament that supports two pollen sacs on its upper part.

Stem

Part of a plant that holds up the leaves or the reproductive structures

Stigma

Upper part of the female reproductive apparatus of a flower. The receptor of pollen, it connects with the ovary.

Storage organ

Part of a plant that consumes sugars or functions to store sugars. Examples are stems, roots, and fruit.

Thallus

Plantlike body of brown seaweed. Also the long, rigid part that holds up the reproductive structures of some fungi.

Thylakoid

Small, flat sac that makes up part of the internal membrane of a chloroplast. Site where solar energy is transformed into chemical energy as part of the process of photosynthesis.

Tissue

Group of identical cells with the same function

Tuber

Modified, thickened underground stem where the plant accumulates reserves of food substances

Vascular

Describes plants with a complex structure and highly organized cells for transporting water and nutrients to all parts of the plant

Xerophyte

Plant that grows in deserts and other dry environments

Xylem

Part of a plant's vascular system. It transports water and minerals from the roots to the rest of the plant.

Index

P

Papaver rhoeas: *See* field poppy
paper production, 76-77
parasitism
    fungus, 84
    plant, 64-65
parrot feather (Myriophyllum aquaticum), 10
pathogenic fungus, 88-89
peach, 54
phaeophyte, 20
phloem
    angiosperms, 9
    leaves, 49
    root systems, 41
    stems, 43
    wood, 44-45
photosynthesis, 16-17
    algae, 20
    cactus, 68
    green revolution, 4-5
    leaves, 12, 48
    start, 37
    tree, 15
    water plants, 10
phycocolloide, 26
phyllotaxis, 46
pine, 56, 57
pine cone: *See* cone
pine nut, 57
Pinus longaeva: *See* bristlecone pine
pitcher plant, 61
plant
    angiosperms, 9
    aquatic plants, 10-11
    Bromeliads, 62
    bud: *See* bud
    cactus, 68-69
    carnivorous: *See* carnivorous plant
    cells, 16-17
    cellulose, 16
    classification, 8-9, 50
    common characteristics, 8
    conifers: *See* conifer

    dioecious, 9
    energy source, 16
    environmental dangers, 5
    epiphytes, 62-63, 64-65
    evolutionary adaptations, 12-13, 65
    first true leaf, 37
    first twenty days, 37
    flower development, 37
    flowerless, 56
    giant, 13
    green revolution, 4-5
    growth rate, 7
    gymnosperms, 9
    history, 5
    hormones, 36
    lack of chlorophyll, 65
    lack of movement, 8
    land conquest, 12
    leaves: *See* leaf
    life cycle, 38-39
    medicinal, 78-79
    monocotyledons (monocots), 9
    naked seed (gnetophyta; gymnosperma), 9
    nearest relatives, 6
    number of species, 4, 8
    parasitic, 64-65
    photosynthesis: *See* photosynthesis
    pines: *See* pine
    poisonous: *See* poisonous plant
    pollination: *See* pollination
    root system, 12, 32-33
    seedless, 8
    seeds: *See* seed
    skin membrane, 12
    stemless, 13
    stems, 42-43
    tissues, 16-17
    tomato, 72-73
    toxic: *See* poisonous plant
    trees: *See* tree
    veined, 46
    water, 10-11
    wetland, 11
plant stem, 42-43
    cactus, 68

    See also tree trunk
pneumatophore, 11
poison hemlock (Conium maculatum), 70
poison ivy (Toxicodendron radicans), 71
poisonous fungus, 86-87
poisonous mushroom, 84-85, 87
poisonous plant, 70-71
pollination, 52-53
    plants with seeds, 38
Polygonum sp.: *See* knotweed
pome, 54
poppy, field: *See* field poppy
potato, common, 42
pressing, olive oil production, 75
psilophyta, 8
pulp, paper, 76

Q-R

Quercus sp.: *See* oak
recaulescence, 46
raceme, 66
red cabbage, 46
red marine algae (Rhodomela sp.), 8
red spider mite (Tetranychus turkestani),
    tomatoes, 72
reproduction
    algae, 22-23
    ferns, 32-33
    flowers, 38-39
    mosses, 31
    mushrooms, 85
    pollination, 52-53
    seedless, 8
    seeds, 36-37
    sexual, 9
    yeast, 91
Rhizopus nigricans: *See* black bread mold
Rhodomela sp.: *See* red marine algae
rhodophyte, 21
rice, 4
Ricinus communis: *See* castor bean
root system, 40-41